★ ★ ★

MAKING SODA
at home

★ ★ ★

MAKING SODA AT HOME

★ ★ ★

MASTERING THE CRAFT OF CARBONATION

JEREMY BUTLER

Quarry Books
100 Cummings Center, Suite 406L
Beverly, MA 01915

quarrybooks.com • quarryspoon.com

First published in the United States of America in
2014 by
Quarry Books, a member of
Quarto Publishing Group USA Inc.
100 Cummings Center
Suite 406-L
Beverly, Massachusetts 01915-6101
Telephone: (978) 282-9590
Fax: (978) 283-2742
www.quarrybooks.com
Visit www.QuarrySPOON.com and help us cele-
brate food and culture one spoonful at a time!

10 9 8 7 6 5 4 3 2 1

ISBN: 978-1-59253-913-0

Digital edition published in 2014
eISBN: 978-1-62788-036-7

Library of Congress Cataloging-in-Publication Data

Butler, Jeremy, B.S.
  Making soda at home : mastering the craft
of carbonation / Jeremy Butler.
     pages cm
  Includes index.
  ISBN 978-1-59253-913-0
  1. Carbonated beverages--Amateurs' manuals. 2.
Soft drinks--Amateurs' manuals. I. Title.
  TP630.B87 2014
  641.87'5--dc23
                              2013048662

Book Design: Debbie Berne
Photography: Paul Sobota
Styling: Dana Sobota

Printed in China

In memory of Bradley Allen, whose friendship and encouragement extend well beyond the short 20 years in which they were offered.

CONTENTS

PREFACE

"Wait . . . You make your own pop?" It's a common reaction I get from people who learn of my hobby for the first time. So how did I get here? I was going to be a director. I was going to live in Hollywood. Then a brief no-start in film school taught me that it wasn't "what you know," it's "who you know," and as it turned out, I didn't know anybody. Having to pull my stolen car out of a Compton tow yard only further tarnished the dream and helped me realize I didn't belong there. Moreover, I needed the promise of something more than being a waiter after graduation.

I discussed at length my predicament with my longtime friend Brad, who was at that time also trying to switch gears in school. He told me that he just needed to win the lottery so that he didn't have to worry about money and he could just focus on learning and doing whatever he wanted. Neither of us being gamblers, we understood the guarantee of that never happening. The discussion turned to the next best thing: being our own bosses and owning a business. I must have gotten carried away with the DIY attitude when I posited the idea of a soda shop where we could make our own flavors of soda and ice cream. I don't know where that came from. I had never made soda flavors before and had done very little with homemade ice cream. He killed the daydreaming session early and told me to slow down and look into food science as a major. He thought I would enjoy it, so I took his advice and he was right. I've never looked back.

I've always played with my food. I remember as a kid making my own recipe for single-serve microwave brownies and peanut butter cups in my mother's kitchen. I also like to do things sometimes as a "proof of concept." The "I'll bet I can . . ." turns into "I need to . . . so I can move on and think about something else." So one day, sitting in a chemistry class and discussing weak acids, namely carbonic acid, I thought to myself that armed with my Chem 105 knowledge, I could make my own soda and do it well. I also wanted to go old school and use actual roots to flavor my root beer. That's when it started to snowball. Always trying to better my batches, I started writing my blog (homemadesodaexpert.blogspot .com), and that has brought me here.

On my journey, I have read the handful of books available on homemade soda and I have noticed that each one seems to focus more on one method of soda making than on a range of methods or techniques. Some books have recipes for fermentation but not much advice on other matters. Other books are just collections of syrup recipes that don't have much advice on adaptation. They are good books, to be sure, and they contain some really great recipes. I recommend them for any soda maker's library as much as anything else. However, there needed to be something a bit more all-encompassing. Enter the Expert. There are a handful of principles employed in this book that other books sort of gloss over or touch on only briefly. The craft of carbonation is truly a blend of science and art. Grasping these principles is what really allows one to understand and improve one's craft.

INTRODUCTION

While this may not be the end-all, be-all homemade soda book, its intent is to be a handbook for beginners, to guide them to become masters. The key to really mastering home soda making is to understand the science. Armed with that, there may be mistakes in the occasional batch, but knowing what went wrong and why is the first step toward warding off discouragement and giving up on the hobby altogether. I've tried to keep the technical stuff to a minimum, but as a trained scientist, it's sometimes hard to do. Fortunately, the science included in the first couple of chapters isn't a full-out college chemistry course; there are only a handful of principles to grasp and they are pretty straightforward. For anyone who wants to skip directly to the recipes, that's certainly doable. It might be more of a rough road if there's a lot of trial and error, but it's doable.

Keep in mind that this is more than just a recipe book. In fact, the recipes here are not as fancy or avant-garde as those that can be found elsewhere. They were intentionally designed that way. Unlike other recipes, however, they are adaptable for the various methods of carbonation in order to bring into focus the possibilities of adaptation. Lots of people like their ginger ale a little tarter, while lots of others like theirs with a little more bite to it. There's nothing wrong with changing up the ingredients a bit to suit individual tastes.

The recipes themselves all have very similar ingredients and methods. To keep the repetition to a minimum, the full technique for each of the three possible methods is given as a recipe template in the opening chapters. These templates are meant for reference in using the actual recipes in Chapter 4. These individual recipes are all scaled to 1-gallon (3.8 liter) batch sizes. I believe that this is a good size because it can easily be scaled up for a 5-gallon (19 liter) keg or scaled down for a siphon. A fermented batch will fit nicely in two store-bought 2-liter bottles, or a batch of syrup will be enough for four 1-liter home carbonated bottles. It is a very convenient and versatile batch size.

Likely the time will come when the 1-gallon batches in these recipes aren't quite enough to serve everyone during a party or get-together, which is why I've included a section on serving soda, a subject that few other books dare to touch on. Having a "soda fountain" at home doesn't have to break the bank. With a little modification, the same equipment used for draft beer at home can be used to pour draft soda.

And finally, at the end of this book I've included some little science projects to illustrate some of the science background of making soda for those who need a little more of a hands-on approach. These can be used just to get a grip on the concepts and to better understand personal preference, or they can be used for the kiddies' science fair. Inexpensive equipment for these projects can be found online without much trouble, so they shouldn't be very far out of reach for most people.

I've described my soda-making hobby a few times already as a journey. With that, I don't believe for one second that this book is the end of the journey. There are many more recipes to write and many more stories to share. Whether that be on my blog or in book form again remains to be seen, but I welcome all to join me in making the world a little more bubbly in their own individual way.

one

THE BASICS OF HOMEMADE SODA

Making soda at home is not only fun and rewarding to the taste buds, but it's also a hobby that never fails to dazzle friends, family, and acquaintances. Though it's a mystery to many, the science behind carbonation is a matter of a few basic chemistry principles. Homemade soda can be as easy as mixing a few ingredients or as complicated as setting up a pressurized carbonating and serving system. Once the basic principles are understood, the possibilities are endless. With a little research and some experimentation, anyone can learn to master the craft of carbonation.

For the beginning homemade soda maker, it's important to explore a number of different recipes to get a feel for what equipment is needed. Perhaps more important is understanding what fancy gimmicks and gadgets are unnecessary before spending the money on them. For the most basic soda making, the only necessary equipment is something to mix it up with and a glass to drink it from. Making an early decision on how "all in" one wants to go with the hobby can pay off in the long run. Otherwise, it can snowball into something really complicated: buying bottles, caps, cappers, bottling/fermenting buckets, jugs, carboys, kegs, draft systems, spare refrigerators or freezers, or maybe even building a dedicated brew room with a walk-in cooler. It sounds crazy, but it's been known to happen to even the best weekend hobbyists.

The popularity of homemade soda has shot up in the past couple of years with an increased interest in all things DIY and a backlash against unpronounceable commercial ingredients, aided by the heavily marketed countertop carbonators now available in local big box stores. While these machines seem like recent feats of modern technology, they are very similar to the basic seltzer siphons that have been around for close to a century. The science certainly hasn't changed—just the marketing and availability. The benefits to these countertop gadgets are that they have compact, sleek designs and are easy to use. However, despite their marketing as money savers, they are likely not the least expensive option in the long run.

SODA'S THREE MAIN COMPONENTS

In its simplest form, soda is a blend of three key ingredients: carbonated water, a sweetener, and a flavor. Anything beyond that, such as the addition of fruit pieces, caffeine, or vitamins, is just embellishment.

Water becomes carbonated when carbon dioxide (CO_2) dissolves into it. This can be done slowly with yeast, or it can be done quickly with pressurized CO_2. Either method has its pros and cons.

The sweetener can be anything from sugar to acesulfame potassium. The sweetener appropriate for any given recipe will depend greatly on a number of factors: carbonation method, final desired flavor, available equipment, budget, nutritional considerations, and availability of the sweetener.

Flavor can be almost anything under the sun. It could be added in the form of extracts, juices, herbs, syrups, spices, or whatever is available. If it has a flavor, chances are it can be made into a soda. Traditional recipes have used just about everything from tree bark to celery. The biggest adventure with this hobby is, "Can I carbonate that?" I find myself asking that question about nearly everything I see in the produce aisle. I've even had questions from others about carbonating items as strange as milk and gravy.

CARBONATED WATER

Carbonated water, or carbonic acid, is simply carbon dioxide dissolved into water. The solubility of carbon dioxide in water—in other words, how much carbonation a soda has—is dependent on three factors: pressure, temperature, and other solutes.

With increased pressure, gases become more soluble in a liquid. Pressure is a measure of molecular collisions, so with increased collisions, there's more mingling of CO_2 and water, which equates to a higher rate of combining to form carbonic acid.

SCIENCE OF SODA

In early chemistry classes, it was hard to imagine gases dissolving into liquids. However, it can be seen in various everyday things. When a solution changes temperature or pressure, then the gas's solubility changes and it can be seen escaping. Consider a glass of cold water left on the counter that eventually warms and has bubbles clinging to the side. This is air that was dissolved in the cold water but came out of solution as it warmed.

The solubility of CO_2 in water also increases as temperature decreases. Ever wonder why a warm soda will be more likely to fizz over when opened than a cold one? It's because a warm soda can't hold carbonation as readily as a cold one. Just as pressure is a measure of molecular motion in the form of collisions, temperature is a measure of molecular motion in terms of rate of speed. More pressure causes more mingling of the molecules, so it favors a higher rate of combining. Higher temperature speeds up molecular motion, so it favors a higher rate of breaking apart.

The third factor that plays a role in solubility is the presence of other solutes. If something else is dissolved in the water, its carbonation capacity is reduced. This can be a challenge that home brewers of beer often struggle with when making soda for the first time. It can seem much more difficult to carbonate a soda than a beer because soda has such a high sugar level. Likewise, a soda with a higher sugar content will lose carbonation once opened much faster than a lower-sugar soda. In chemistry terms, when a solute dissolves into a solvent, the solute molecules interact directly with the molecules of the solvent. As such, the water molecules that are preoccupied with interactions of other solutes simply don't have the capacity to interact with the CO_2.

SCIENCE OF SODA

To better understand this, we must think of the soda as a system in equilibrium: $CO_2 + H_2O = H_2CO_3$. A chemical reaction like this should be recognizable from a high school chemistry class. What's not often remembered, though, is that some chemical reactions, such as this one, are actually a two-way street. Conditions dictate which way the reaction goes. The pressure of CO_2 forces the molecules to intermingle; when the oxygen molecules in the CO_2 approach the hydrogen molecules in the water, they're attracted to each other, and the strength of the attraction tends to pull them away, but they're still closely held by the water's oxygen, so they switch around a bit and attractions are satisfied for a little while, but with enough motion (or heat), these will break up and go back to the way they were before. This is going on constantly within the system, and it comes to equilibrium when the rate of combining is equal to the rate of breaking apart. Now, here's something that's counterintuitive to something everyone has known about soda since they were little kids: Agitation favors equilibrium, regardless of the direction to get there. So to speed up a return to equilibrium, we can shake it up. This will be both a help and a hindrance depending on the situation. If we're trying to carbonate faster and the system is sealed or has pressure on it, we can shake it to get the CO_2 to dissolve. If we're trying to maintain carbonation levels on an open system, we want to minimize agitation by slowing the speed of pouring or pouring down the side of a glass.

SUGAR AND OTHER SWEETENERS

The second important component to soda is some sort of sweetness. Some critics of soda refer to it as "liquid candy." While this may not be too far off base, it doesn't necessarily mean it's a bad thing. Candy is a comfort food that can remind us of our childhood and, likely for most, so is soda. It brings out the child in everyone and holds its fair share of nostalgia. While juice spritzers and unsweetened soda waters certainly have their place and purpose as refreshment, sweetness is a key component to the traditional soda. Though table sugar is the most accessible and is used in most of the recipes here, there are many other sources, for better or for worse.

SUCROSE

We use the term "sugar" most commonly to refer to the disaccharide sucrose. There are numerous other sugars available, but sucrose is the most common and readily available and is ranked second in sweetness only to fructose. It can come from sugar cane or sugar beets. It can be brown, white, powdered, or even liquid.

Cane Sugar Cane sugar is sucrose that is derived from sugar cane. A lot of food companies are touting "all cane sugar" because it looks better on the label than "beet sugar." However, refined beet sugar and refined cane sugar both have the same flavor. Cane sugar is very common, but it can come in different forms.

Granulated White The white granular sugar that so many know and love is common, easily obtainable, has a clean flavor profile, and is relatively inexpensive. In an oversimplified nutshell, it gets to that white crystalline form after several extractions and evaporations have removed the juice from the cane, then the water from the juice, and then the molasses, leaving the white crystals that are so well known and loved.

Brown Brown sugar is granulated sugar to which a certain level of molasses has been added back. Brown sugar is useful in a beverage where a darker caramel flavor is desired, such as in a root beer or cola. It can also be useful in caramel, golden cream soda, and other indulgent flavors.

Turbinado or Raw Raw cane sugar is becoming increasingly available. It is the sugar that is extracted from the first pressing of sugar cane juice. A lot of people are turning to raw sugar and other "premium" ingredients because they fear or disagree with the refining or processing of foods. Other than its status as a more natural alternative, raw sugar has other merits in beverage making. It has a bolder flavor than refined white sugar but is mellower than brown sugar. It adds subtle flavor notes to a beverage that may be overpowered by brown sugar. If more depth of flavor is desired in a root beer without much of a molasses hit, then raw sugar may give just the right touch of flavor.

Molasses Molasses is the syrup that's left over after extracting granulated sugar from the sugar cane. It comes in different grades from mild to bold. This is a great option for a bold flavor for a root beer or cola when there's not a lot of sweetness desired. It can also be used in small amounts with granulated sugar to mimic brown sugar flavor if there isn't any on hand or to obtain a more intense brown sugar flavor than using brown sugar alone.

Beet Sugar As mentioned, cane sugar and beet sugar are nearly identical in flavor. Some tests have shown cane sugar to be superior in some applications, mostly baking and some candy making. Typically manufacturers selling beet sugar to consumers market the product as simply "sugar," which gives them the flexibility to source it from sugar cane or from sugar beets or from a blend of both. In beverages, there's no functional or flavor benefit

Here are various sweeteners used in soda. Clockwise from top left: Invert cane syrup (A), brown sugar (B), turbinado sugar (C), white sugar (D), organic sugar (E), honey (F), corn syrup (G), molasses (H)

in choosing one over the other. If both are available, then price is typically the deciding factor. Brown sugar is not usually made from beets because the refining process takes it straight to the white granular stage, and the resulting molasses is not used for human consumption due to the often unpleasant aroma it carries.

INVERT SUGAR

The sucrose molecule is made up of fructose and glucose, which are both single-molecule sugars on their own. On a scale of perceived sweetness, fructose is the sweetest, followed by sucrose, and third comes glucose. Sucrose is by far the easiest to come by, but a blend of the three can be made by breaking up some of the sucrose into fructose and glucose using an enzyme or an acid. Invertase is an enzyme that breaks the bonds and makes up this blend and is often used in candy making. The blend is called "invert sugar," as a reference to polarized light tests,

in comparison to normal sugar. It can't be seen without the aid of scientific equipment, but it helps to know this so that the terminology isn't as confusing.

Many have questioned the effort of making an invert sugar blend. Simply put, more sweetness can be achieved out of the same amount of sugar (by weight). Using an invert sugar is also an easy way of slowing crystallization of syrups if they are to be stored for any period of time by contributing a variation of size and shape to the molecules in solution.

Inverting Sucrose Syrup Another way to make invert sugar is to heat the sugar in the presence of an acid such as cream of tartar (tartaric acid), vinegar, or citric acid. Cream of tartar has a neutral taste that is good for most herbal or indulgent recipes. Citric acid in granular form or naturally found in fruit juices has a characteristically fruity tang and is best used for recipes that have at least some sort of fruity component. Vinegar has its own unique sour bite that can be delicious in some recipes yet unwelcome in others; used carefully, it can make a very refreshing beverage. Recipes for inverting sugar are readily found in various places online, but here is the simplified version that I use.

> 2 cups sugar (about 1 pound, or 455 g)
> 1 cup (235 ml) water
> ¼ teaspoon cream of tartar or granular citric acid
> *or* 2 tablespoons (28 ml) lemon juice
> *or* 2 tablespoons (28 ml) white vinegar

1. Combine all three ingredients in a saucepan until all the sugar is wet. Any sugar that is still dry can easily burn. **(A)**

2. Without stirring, heat the mixture to boiling and allow it to simmer until it reaches 240°F (116°C). This usually takes about 20 minutes, but when doubling the recipe the time doubles as well. Some recipes say to use a wet pastry brush to brush the sugar on the sides of the pan back into the solution, but since this won't be used for candy making, it's not that critical. **(B)**

3. If it starts to darken, immediately add ¼ cup (60 ml) more water and remove from the heat. A properly inverted sugar should have a strong, biting sweetness similar to honey and be very thick and difficult to pour when cooled. Adding extra water just after removing it from the heat should keep it easier to work with for beverage making. **(C)**

Honey Invertase is the same enzyme that bees use to convert the sugars in flower nectar, and as such, honey is an invert sugar. Honey can also lend floral notes to a beverage where it is needed. Cola often has a floral component that can be mimicked with a strong floral honey if actual flowers are not available. Since the sugars in honey have been nearly completely inverted, its sweetness is more intense than sucrose, and its source lends delicate floral notes that give a honey its characteristic flavor.

Honey can be used for a truly artisanal soda, but it can get expensive if that's the primary sweetener.

The delicate floral notes can fade as honey gets old or gets abused with heat if adding to a syrup. Another thing to keep in mind is that honey can harbor wild yeasts that may cause a fermented soda to develop off flavors. Such is the nature of natural ingredients. On that same note, don't give honey to children younger than 1 year (some doctors recommend not giving honey to children younger than 2 years). Other than that, I'll leave the discussion of giving honey-sweetened soda (or any soda) to infants well enough alone.

CORN SYRUP

Corn syrup is a slurry of cornstarch wherein the starches have been enzymatically hydrolyzed into sugars. Most corn syrups are not completely hydrolyzed, but consist of small chains with links that fall into a certain size range. They will have different properties depending on how broken up the chains are. The corn syrup off the shelf at the grocery store is sort of an "all-purpose" blend of different types of syrups. The main component of these is likely high-fructose syrup.

High-Fructose Corn Syrup (HFCS) High-fructose corn syrup (HFCS) is a sweetener that is not often necessarily available to most consumers. It is used in most commercial sodas and thus merits some discussion. It's basically a corn syrup that has had some of the glucose converted via enzymes into fructose. It was meant to mimic the sweetness profile of sucrose syrup. Some people can perceive a flavor difference in sodas made from it compared to the same sodas made from sugar, and some people can't.

HFCS has received some bad publicity in the past few years. I have issues with those on both sides of the argument. I don't think it should be vilified as the source of all ills in our food supply. It's in a wide variety of foods, that's for sure. That doesn't mean it's an industry conspiracy. The truth is that it's in there for a number of purposes. It can be a sweetener, a browning agent in baked goods, a humectant to keep foods moist, a yeast food, a preservative, and

so on. It's also inexpensive. It's also not well established that it causes diseases any more readily than cane sugar. So those people avoiding it at all costs for fear of any perceived poisonous effects may be misguided if they're just switching sugars rather than eating less sugar overall.

On the other hand, it's still in a wide variety of foods and we shouldn't take that lightly. Droughts and other events with heavy impacts on corn should highlight our country's dangerous reliance on multi-use single crops. Did we learn nothing from the Irish potato famine? Furthermore, portion sizes and over-indulgence are out of control. From its infancy into recent decades, soda has been considered a novelty and a treat. When the eco-friendly returnable bottle from local bottlers gave way to lighter-weight PET and more centralized bottling plants, along with a move from premix to post-mix fountains, larger volumes of soda became cheaper to obtain. Now more than ever, with our constant on-the-go lifestyle, soda is a staple at every meal. It's no longer in a 6½-ounce (190 ml) bottle, it's in a 64-ounce (1.8 L) refillable cup that we can take with us anywhere in our gigantic cupholder in the SUV.

Therein lies the danger of HFCS, but the danger would remain the same if all sodas were made with cane sugar. Would anyone spoon out a full cup of sugar onto the plate at any meal? If not, then why are we consuming that much sugar when we guzzle that 64-ounce (1.8 L) mega mug? That's food for thought.

Other As mentioned, there are other corn syrups that are used in the food industry, and these are usually mixed with HFCS to create the all-purpose product we buy for use in baking or candy making at home. These other types are likely not available to the average consumer. They come in different viscosities with varying levels of sweetness for numerous applications. They are usually thick and less sweet than HFCS, which make them difficult to handle and less desirable for beverage making.

AGAVE NECTAR

Agave nectar is a syrup of fructose and glucose and is sweeter than sugar because of its very high fructose content. It has gained popularity among those concerned with blood sugar levels because the body's response in terms of spikes in blood sugar is much slower, mainly because the body has to convert the fructose to glucose in order to use it.

It is derived from the agave plant, the same type of plant that is distilled to make tequila. The plants used to make it take 5 to 7 years to reach maturity, at which point the cores or leaves are removed to extract the syrup. For beverages, it can be used in a manner similar to honey, though its limited availability can make it somewhat expensive.

NON-NUTRITIVE

Non-nutritive sweeteners are substances that taste sweet but contribute no calories. These have usually been limited to artificial sweeteners, but there is great interest and research into natural sources of non-caloric sweetness. They can be used in place of sugar in beverages to make a diet soda; however, figuring out how to use them can be tricky when trying to convert a recipe. Often they're used in such small amounts that a precise kitchen scale is needed to measure them out in grams or even milligrams. When converting recipes to diet soda, remember that these are not fermentable, so sugar is still required for yeast to create carbonation. That can be used to an advantage, though. Once all the added sugar is fermented out, fermentation ceases and there is no longer any risk of exploding bottles.

Artificial Sweeteners There are many artificial sweeteners on the market, though some are not readily available to the average consumer. Anyone who reads labels on diet drinks will recognize their names. They are often touted as many times sweeter than sugar, so they are used at very low percentages. When used at higher percentages, they can begin to taste bitter to some and leave an aftertaste. The most common are saccharin, aspartame, sucralose, and acesulfame potassium.

Saccharin has been around for more than a hundred years, though it didn't find much use until the late 1950s. In the United States, it is the sweetener in Sweet'N Low. (Sweet'N Low in Canada contains cyclamate because saccharin is banned in Canada, whereas cyclamates are banned in the United States.) It is usually used as sodium saccharin.

Aspartame consists of two amino acids: aspartic acid and phenylalanine. NutraSweet is a recognizable brand name of aspartame. It does not hold up well to heating, so it shouldn't be heated in a syrup.

Sucralose has become increasingly prominent since its approval in the United States in 1998. It is a chlorinated sucrose molecule that the body does not metabolize. It is marketed under the Splenda name. It is heat stable, so it can be found in the grocery store along with other baking ingredients. Often, the commercially available version is mostly maltodextrin so that it can be substituted for sugar in recipes cup for cup, and this makes it easy to convert any soda recipe to a diet soda recipe with little effort.

Acesulfame potassium is also known as acesulfame K or simply ace K. Like sucralose, it holds up well to heat, but it is not as widely available. It is usually used in conjunction with other sweeteners because it is known to have a bitter aftertaste.

Stevia The extract from the several species of stevia plants, known as rebaudioside A, is one of the very few natural, non-nutritive sweeteners and has seen great success in the few years since its approval in the United States for use in food. There are many different versions and some have unpleasant aftertastes, but its use is similar to the artificial sweeteners. It is mostly available in health food stores due to its approval as a dietary supplement rather than a food additive, but there are an increasing number of stevia-based sweeteners that are showing up on grocery store shelves.

Monk Fruit Extract Another natural sweetener that is gaining popularity and grocery store shelf space is monk fruit extract. The monk fruit is originally from Southeast Asia and has been used there for many years. The fruit itself contains some unpleasant aromas, so the extract is used instead of the fruit pulp. Like sucralose, it is typically sold on a maltodextrin carrier and usually comes in single-serve packets. For soda making, its availability and its price tag make it best suited for small batches.

FLAVORS

Flavor is the third main component of a soda. I like to categorize the basic flavors of soda into three different groups: fruity, indulgent, and herbal. Fruity sodas are characterized by the tartness that comes from the citric acid naturally found in fruit. Indulgent flavors are typically sweet without much tartness and include flavors such as vanilla, chocolate, and caramel. Herbal flavors come from steeped herbs, roots, and flowers. These often lack tartness as well but commonly have cooling notes similar to mint and wintergreen.

FRUITY

Fruity flavors can come from extracts, from fruit juices, or from infusions. Extracts found in the baking section at any local grocery store are easy additions to basic syrup. Juices are readily available and have well-rounded sweetness, acidity, color, and flavor. Using juice can sometimes be expensive when making syrups, because they already have a high water content that typically needs to be boiled down, which can destroy the flavor. Juice concentrates are best for making syrups, where most of the work of removing the water has already been done under lower pressure and at lower temperature conditions than can be achieved in a home kitchen. This preserves their flavor and offers a better-quality product with a syrup. Single-strength juices are best used for fermented or straight carbonation recipes. Fruit infusions, accomplished by soaking fruit in still water, can have the same drawbacks as juices when making soda, and so these are best done with low-sugar recipes that are carbonated directly.

INDULGENT

Indulgent flavors are what we think of as decadent desserts. These include things like chocolate, vanilla, and caramel. These flavors typically come from extracts, but they can come from steeping the raw ingredients, such as malted grains, cocoa nibs, or vanilla beans. Cream soda is a good example of something that falls into this category.

HERBAL

For centuries, roots and herbs have been steeped to make tonics and teas for medicinal purposes. Under storage, these would sometimes carbonate themselves from the action of wild yeasts, and these were some of the early precursors to modern-day sodas. Root beer, cola, and ginger ale are prominent members of this family.

ACIDS

Acids are important, yet often overlooked, components to flavor. The most commonly used acids for soda flavors are citric acid, phosphoric acid, and acetic acid from vinegar.

Citric acid has a tartness that is characteristic of fresh fruit. It is destroyed by high heat, so a fruit syrup that has lost its tartness can be made to taste fresh again by adding some citric acid.

Phosphoric acid is one of the characteristic flavors of cola. It can be difficult to obtain and should be used with caution. It is partially responsible for the placement of sodas on most dentists' blacklists.

Acetic acid is what gives vinegar its characteristic bite. It is not common in commercial sodas, but historically it plays its role in beverages called shrubs that can be surprisingly refreshing, despite the fact that drinking vinegar can seem repulsive to some.

NATURAL CARBONATION

SCIENCE

To carbonate naturally, yeast is added to the uncarbonated soda base and it is bottled in something that will contain the pressure. Yeasts metabolize sugar into ethyl alcohol and carbon dioxide. As the pressure builds, the solubility of CO_2 increases and creates carbonation. On a molecular basis, equal amounts of carbon dioxide and alcohol are created for the amount of sugar consumed. When adequate carbonation is reached, the soda is moved from an ambient temperature to a refrigerated temperature. This makes the yeast less active, and it eventually settles out. Fermentation doesn't stop, but it does slow down significantly. Natural carbonation recipes work very well with ingredients that are steeped or with recipes that include fruit juices. All the recipes in this book include a yeast nutrient. This is optional, but sometimes if yeasts are stressed or if the ingredients don't have everything needed to keep the yeasts going, yeasts will produce other compounds that can lead to off odors and flavors. The most common ones that I've experienced are, first, a rotten egg smell, which comes from the yeasts not having enough nitrogen to reproduce. The second that I've encountered is a medicine-like or adhesive bandage flavor, which comes from residual chlorine, either from chlorinated tap water or from using bleach as a sanitizer. These can be lessened or eliminated by being careful with ingredients and sanitizers along with using a yeast nutrient.

BASIC RECIPE

This recipe will serve as a template for all the recipes to follow. These are the basic steps when making a fermented soda. For best results, ferment at a constant temperature around 75°F (24°C). After completion, it should be ready to drink as soon as it is cold, but a longer period of refrigeration will allow the yeast to settle out and keep the flavor a little cleaner. This is not necessary, and sometimes the carbonation will bring it back up when the bottle is opened anyway, and that's normal. Some recipes will take longer than others: The average time is about 24 hours, but I've had some take as little as 12 hours and others take as long as 72 hours.

For a 1-gallon (3.8 L) basic fermented recipe, here is what is needed:

> Stockpot
> Fine-mesh sieve
> Funnel
> Bottles with caps
> 1 gallon (3.8 L) water
> Flavoring ingredients
> 2¼ cups (450 g) sugar (non-nutritive sweeteners will not ferment)
> ⅛ teaspoon Champagne yeast
> 1 g yeast nutrient

1. **Brewing:** The roots/herbs are steeped first in a stockpot with as much water as possible to extract as much flavor as possible before sugar is added. **(A)**

2. **Straining:** The brewed solids are filtered out through a fine-mesh sieve. **(B)** A muslin bag used for tea making can be used for finer ingredients, and a coffee filter can be used for even finer ingredients. Filter gradually. A finer filter will clog faster and need changing more often.

3. **Sweetening:** Add the sugar and any other flavoring components, such as extracts or juices. **(C)**

4. **Pitching:** After the mixture has cooled to room temperature, the yeast can be added. Hydrate the yeast in about ¼ cup (60 ml) warm water with a drop of molasses or some extra sugar as a starter. When dissolved, it should begin to bubble, and the yeast can be added to the room temperature mixture. **(D)** To determine alcohol content later, it is important to take a hydrometer reading before bottling (see step 7).

5. **Bottling:** After the yeast is mixed thoroughly, add the yeast nutrient, and then the mixture can be bottled and sealed. **(E)** Allow to ferment at room

temperature. Plastic bottles are best for fermented recipes because they can be tested for pressure by squeezing them. Plastic bottles also hold higher pressures without exploding.

6. **Testing for completion:** When the bottles have become stiff and incompressible, carbonation has reached its optimum level. **(F)** From this point, the bottles can be refrigerated and will be ready to drink when cold. It is important to remember that refrigerating does not stop fermentation; it only slows it. Drink within a few days.

7. **Alcohol content:** Determining alcohol content requires comparing a hydrometer reading taken before fermentation (see step 5) to a hydrometer reading taken after fermentation. Using a hydrometer is as simple as floating it in a liquid and reading the number at the surface.

ALCOHOL CONTENT

It's a common misconception that the fermentation for soda doesn't produce any alcohol. The truth is that it produces what some would consider a negligible amount of alcohol, typically less than 0.5% by volume. The difference between fermenting for beer or wine and fermenting for soda is the extent of fermentation and the buildup of pressure. Beer or wine is fermented in a carboy or demijohn that allows the carbon dioxide to escape, and fermentation continues until all the sugar is consumed. Soda is fermented in a tightly sealed container that captures all the carbon dioxide released by the yeast and builds pressure to carbonate. A highly carbonated soda could likely build up enough alcohol to be 0.7 to 0.8%, but at that point they tend to foam like volcanoes when they're opened, and anything beyond that becomes explosively dangerous, particularly in glass bottles. With fermentation also continuing slowly during refrigeration, sodas are best consumed within a few days. For anyone who tends not to go through a bottle of soda very quickly, fermenting is probably not the best choice for carbonation.

USING A HYDROMETER, IF DESIRED

Even the slightest amount of alcohol can be a concern to some, for health or religious reasons. To be sure of a soda's alcohol content or lack thereof, the easiest measure is the hydrometer. This measures a beverage's specific gravity. Comparing the specific gravity before fermentation to the specific gravity after fermentation gives a comparison of how much sugar has been fermented out. A conversion factor determines the overall alcohol content. A hydrometer will typically come with specific instructions, but this is generally how it is used.

Equipment:
Beer or wine hydrometer
Graduated cylinder *or* bottle at least tall enough for the hydrometer to be fully submerged
Notebook to record and compare readings

1. After mixing up the beverage completely (ensure that all the sugar is dissolved and well mixed), fill the graduated cylinder with the mix and place the hydrometer into the cylinder. Some hydrometers are meant to be read at the top of the meniscus, and some are meant to be read at the bottom. The important number is the difference between the readings, so whichever way it's done needs to be consistent.

2. Record the number on the scale at the surface of the liquid; it will likely be in the range of 1.050 to 1.080. If the hydrometer has a "Potential Alcohol" scale, that's an easier number to record and work with, though it may be imprecise for soda-making purposes.

3. After the yeast has adequately carbonated the beverage, take a sample big enough to fit into the graduated cylinder. This will need to be de-carbonated by shaking it and releasing the pressure repeatedly. If carbonation is left in the sample, bubbles may form on the hydrometer, making it rise and skewing the results. Repeat the procedure for reading the hydrometer and record the number.

4. With the numbers on the "Potential Alcohol" scale, one must simply subtract the final reading from the original reading to get the correct alcohol percentage. If there is only a specific gravity scale, then the difference must be multiplied by 131. For example, my grape soda started at 1.080 and ended at 1.076. So, 1.080 − 1.076 = 0.004, and 0.004 × 131 = 0.524. This means that I ended up with just over 0.5% alcohol by volume (ABV).

FERMENTING IN GLASS BOTTLES

Glass bottles are common in home brewing because they are almost infinitely reusable. They also hold a certain level of charm and nostalgia. A steady supply of re-cappable bottles can be sourced from friends who drink craft or imported beer or imported sodas in glass bottles. Swing top bottles are also handy, but they are harder to come by used. Both bail top and crown cap finish bottles can be purchased new at any good home-brew supply store. There is some inherent uncertainty about bottling in glass. One can never really tell whether the carbonation is complete without opening the bottle. When opened, the fermentation gets set back a little bit, since carbonation is dependent so much on pressure. Add to this the possibility that one bottle may ferment faster than the next, and there is the likelihood of exploding bottles.

FERMENTING IN PET BOTTLES

Clean plastic (PET) soda bottles are recommended for fermenting soda. It's easy to check the pressure by squeezing them, and their elasticity allows them to withstand higher pressures before exploding. They aren't as reusable as glass, as they do eventually wear out, and they are susceptible to scratches that are harder to clean and sanitize. They also lack the charm and crafty presentation that comes from a classic glass bottle. Bottling in glass is certainly possible, but for the sake of safety, it's always best practice to have some test bottles around to check the carbonation levels. Whether these are smaller glass bottles that can be opened to test or PET bottles that can be squeezed doesn't really matter.

KEG FERMENTATION

Fermenting can be done in a keg just as well as it can be done in a bottle. Some home-brew kegs have trouble sealing at low pressures, so it is often helpful to pressurize the headspace first to get a good seal. Attaching a pressure gauge will give an indication of when the fermentation is complete and the soda is ready to be refrigerated. The challenge again here is going through soda fast enough before the fermentation goes too far. Most home-brew kegs are 5 gallons, which equates to almost ten 2-liter bottles. This is enough for a good-sized party but probably too much for a family to go through in a short period of time.

FORCE CARBONATION

SCIENCE

Force carbonation is the process of introducing CO_2 from sources other than yeast. Truth be told, the chemical process of "forcing" CO_2 into solution is the same as for natural carbonation, but it is most often faster and much easier to control.

COMMERCIAL CARBONATOR

A motorized carbonator is what is used on post-mix systems in food service settings. This allows for a virtually continuous flow of carbonated water that is mixed separately with syrup in the nozzle of the fountain. The carbonator is basically a holding tank where high pressure CO_2 (100 psi) fills the headspace and the motor forces water into the tank. The higher pressure and relatively large surface area carbonate the water quickly before it is fed out to the fountain. This type of carbonator can sometimes be purchased used from restaurants going out of business, but it requires some technical know-how along with dedicated space and plumbing to set it up correctly.

DRY ICE

Dry ice is frozen carbon dioxide and sublimates at -109.3°F (-78.5°C). People love to use this to carbonate drinks at parties because of the haze it gives off. With enough dry ice, sodas can be carbonated, but the process is somewhat inefficient. Liquids carbonate best under pressure, but sealing off a vessel with dry ice inside is dangerous. Dry ice will turn to a gas quicker than it can dissolve into the liquid, so even having the correct amount of dry ice to produce 3 or 4 volumes of carbonation is likely to build up excessive pressure before equilibrium is reached. Another problem with dry ice is that it can sometimes build up a shell of ice around it because of its low surface temperature. The reduction in contact that this causes between the liquid and the gas slows down the absorption of CO_2 even further.

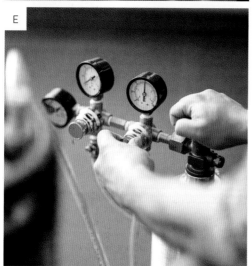

HOME CARBONATORS

Home carbonators such as the SodaStream are simply variations of the classic soda siphon and, in some respects, the keg. In simplest terms, they are all sealed vessels with the ability to inject CO_2.

CARBONATING READY TO DRINK

Force carbonation of a ready-to-drink beverage was the standard at most food service fountains just before bag-in-box post-mix systems were in use. "Home-brew kegs" are actually the secondhand stock of premix soda tanks that have been sold off from the big name bottlers. Premix allows some more flexibility when creating a soda with ingredients that are destroyed easily by heat and thus don't work well in a syrup. Force carbonating juices also works well with a premix setup because they already contain so much water. Adding juice to a seltzer only dilutes the carbonation that's already there.

BASIC RECIPE

The template for using a straight carbonation recipe is very similar to that of putting together a fermented recipe. The difference is that instead of adding yeast and bottling, the mixed beverage is chilled and carbonated in a keg, siphon, or other appropriate carbonator. These recipes have been kept to 1 gallon (3.8 L) for easy scaling even though that size is not a common size for a carbonating apparatus. A 1-gallon batch can still be carbonated in a 5-gallon (19 L) keg. Though some claim that this method is wasteful, it is actually less wasteful of CO_2 (to say nothing of ingredients) than making a properly carbonated 5-gallon batch and only using 1 gallon.

For a 1-gallon (3.8 L) basic straight carbonated recipe, here is what is needed:

Stockpot
Fine-mesh sieve
Funnel
Keg or soda siphon
Flavoring ingredients
Sugar

1. **Brewing:** The roots/herbs are steeped first in a stockpot with as much water as possible to extract as much flavor as possible before sugar is added. **(A)**

2. **Straining:** The brewed ingredients are filtered out through a fine-mesh sieve. **(B)** A muslin bag

SODAMAKING FAQ

One question that I see come up time and time again is: "How long will it take for my soda to carbonate?" The short answer is: "That depends." It depends on volume, temperature, sugar content, and agitation. If it just pressurizes and is left untouched at room temperature, a 5 gallon (19 L) keg may take weeks to carbonate fully, if it ever gets there at all. On the other hand, an ice cold 1 quart (950 ml) siphon will carbonate almost instantaneously with some shaking.

To carbonate quickly, remember the following:
- Keep things cold.
- Shake vigorously until no more CO_2 enters solution.
- Keep the volume low; even allowing a little extra headspace in a keg can speed things up dramatically.

used for tea making can be used for finer ingredients, and a coffee filter can be used for even finer ingredients.

3. **Sugar addition:** After straining out the roots, the sweetener of choice is added, along with the rest of the water. **(C)**

4. **Filling keg:** With the soda base mixed and sweetened, it is added to the keg or siphon to the appropriate fill level. **(D)**

5. **Pressurizing keg:** A siphon is pressurized with cartridges and the pressure is not adjustable. The small volume will carbonate quickly. A keg will need to be set to the appropriate pressure and allowed to achieve equilibrium before it is fully carbonated. **(E)**

SYRUP + SELTZER

Sodas that are served from a fountain in food service are now usually post-mix, meaning they are mixed at the nozzle after carbonation of the water has taken place. The syrup-plus-seltzer method is also how the classic fountains at corner drugstores were set up. For homemade versions, this method also works well and is the method recommended when using the SodaStream. Water is actually the easiest thing to force carbonate in a keg or siphon because there are no other solutes. Dispensing seltzer on top of syrup is preferred to avoid bubbling over. If mixed by the glass, carbonation is lost with excessive vigorous mixing. If mixed by the bottle, careful procedure can retain most of the carbonation in the seltzer. This method requires the least equipment and investment. A 2-liter (½ gallon) bottle of club soda or seltzer works just as well as something carbonated at home.

BASIC RECIPE

This basic template should be followed for all the subsequent recipes when using a syrup with carbonated water. For optimum carbonation in a bottled soda using this method, it is better to keep the syrup as concentrated as possible to keep the CO_2 in solution until the bottle is sealed. When mixing by the glass, a thinner syrup will mix quickly without much agitation.

The concentration of the syrup may vary from batch to batch depending on how much water is used to steep the flavor ingredients and how long the syrup is boiled down. It's a good idea to measure it out once it's made to know the ratio of syrup to carbonated water to use later on. Most of the recipes here turn out to be a ratio of between 1:3 and 1:7 of syrup to carbonated water, which translates to between 4 cups (950 ml) and 2 cups (475 ml) of syrup respectively. When I make syrup batches that come out to an uneven ratio, I like to add enough extra water to "normalize" the batch for ease of use. A good, quick way to test this on a small scale is to mix a spoonful in a glass with a number of spoonfuls of water. This is an easy way to mix to taste without potentially ruining the entire batch.

For a 1-gallon (3.8 L) basic syrup recipe, here is what is needed:

> Saucepan
> Fine-mesh sieve
> Funnel
> Bottles with caps (or mix by the glass)
> Water for steeping (about 2 cups [500 ml])
> Flavoring ingredients
> Sugar
> Carbonated water (up to 1 gallon [3.8 L])

1. **Brewing:** The roots/herbs are usually steeped first in a stockpot with as much water as possible to extract optimum flavor before sugar is added. **(A)**

2. **Straining:** The particulates are filtered out through a fine-mesh sieve. **(B)** A muslin bag used for tea making can be used for finer ingredients, and a coffee filter can be used for even finer ingredients.

3. **Adding sugar:** After straining, sugar is added and the mix is cooked to a desired consistency. **(C)** Add any flavor extracts only after the syrup has cooled.

4. **Filling bottles (syrup):** Syrup is added to the glass bottles to the correct ratio. **(D)**

5. **Filling bottles (seltzer):** Cold seltzer water is added to the bottles and filled to capacity. **(E)** Care is taken to ensure there is not too much vigorous mixing of the syrup with the seltzer so as to retain an adequate level of carbonation. The best way to do this is to tilt the bottle and allow the syrup to flow down the side.

6. **Capping (if desired):** Carbonation is best when the bottles are capped before thoroughly mixing. **(F)**

STORAGE OF FINISHED SODA

Commercial sodas are stabilized with preservatives such as sodium benzoate and potassium sorbate so they can sit on a shelf at room temperature without spoiling. These primarily inhibit microbial growth. Microbial spoilage is not the only concern in relation to the shelf life of soda. Chemical reactions continue on with or without the aid of microbes. Flavor tends to fade or change, and even in unstabilized home sodas, these reactions sometimes occur before any microbial spoilage occurs. It is best to store homemade sodas refrigerated. Fermented sodas will keep for a few days to a couple of weeks in the refrigerator, while force-carbonated sodas can keep for weeks or months. Outside the refrigerator, fermented sodas will likely explode in as little as a few days, whereas force-carbonated sodas may keep for a few weeks before flavor change occurs, or they may start to ferment spontaneously. This largely depends on ingredients and sanitation techniques.

Storage should be a consideration when sharing homemade sodas. Instructions should be given to a friend or neighbor to keep their gifts refrigerated to avoid the awkward experience of having it explode on their kitchen counter.

Storing syrups can be a great way to store flavors longer, but shelf life largely depends on ingredients, the concentration, and the method by which the syrup was made. An invert syrup will keep longer and be less likely to crystallize than a simple syrup. Syrups can keep for an average of 3 to 6 months in the refrigerator.

When storing sodas, be sure to have a container that will hold pressure. PET bottles that were not designed for carbonated beverages will often start to deform to the point where they will tip over or vent pressure from the cap. Whether force carbonated or fermented, this can mean the difference between a tasty, well carbonated soda and a flat disaster. Even some glass containers were not made for pressure or aren't food-safe at all. Some swing-top bottles were made solely for decoration and are made with very thin glass. I've even seen some in various colors where the glass is actually clear with a colored coating on the inside. While these can be tempting vessels for DIY artisan gifts, it's best to stick with something that was intended for beverage use.

SODAMAKING FAQ

People like to show off their creations, and with the colorful possibilities of fruity, homemade sodas, that's understandable. I see questions come up frequently about where to find clear bottles suitable for soda. In fact, the Bottle Sources portion of my blog is the most viewed post outside of actual recipes. My favorite bottles are 187 ml (6 ½ ounce) champagne bottles. These are available from many homebrew supply stores and they have a classic vintage look to them. Another good option is reusing Mexican beverage bottles. The most popular Mexican beer comes in clear 12 and 7 ounce (355 and 200 ml) bottles, though getting the labels off is a trick. Also look for the Mexican version of the world's favorite cola.

two

DEVELOPING RECIPES

The aim of this book is not the what, but the how, with the intent to be a how-to cookbook rather than simply a recipe book. Many of the recipes here are not fancy culinary masterpieces, but rather solid basic flavored beverages to gain experience beyond the usual. Friends and neighbors frequently ask me, "Can you make [insert flavor here] soda?" Often people will request common flavors such as root beer or ginger ale, for which a brief Internet search will turn up a plethora of recipes. Occasionally, however, some of the requests are for small regional sodas or off-the-wall flavors that don't have established recipes. Developing recipes quickly becomes a necessary skill for an accomplished soda maker.

Adapting recipes could be as simple as adding carbonated water to a favorite still beverage recipe or as complicated as turning a hot baked dessert into a cold refreshing soda. The possibilities are endless. Whenever I adapt a recipe, I like to step back and look at what's already out there. I might take a conglomeration of recipes and look at them for inspiration on what the main flavoring components are and what their amounts are relative to one another. What do they have in common? Which ones have the best reviews?

Recipe development is also an important skill when you are trying to recreate a historic or incomplete recipe. A dash of salt or a pinch of sugar were once perfectly acceptable ways of recording ingredient amounts. Older cookbooks or recipe collections where fermented soda recipes are likely to be found can sometimes be frustratingly vague. Adapting a recipe from conventional to diet may also be a challenge, depending on the desired sweetener and how it interacts with other ingredients. Some testing and tweaking may be required to obtain a desirable diet soda.

KEEPING A NOTEBOOK

One of the most important things to do when developing recipes is to keep a detailed notebook. Sometimes seemingly insignificant details can mean the difference between a soda that is irresistible and one that is passable. It's easy to forget for how long the syrup was cooked or whether the extract was in the amount of ½ teaspoon or ¼ teaspoon. The notebook is not only a place to record recipes and amounts of ingredients, but it's also helpful for making notes on technique, flavor, carbonation, and sweetness. This gives a reference point for future batches with regard to what worked and what didn't. Inevitably, there will be mistakes for better or for worse that will affect the outcome of the finished soda in unexpected ways. When these are not recorded and are later forgotten, they are mistakes that are repeated time and time again. A spiral-bound notebook is a very inexpensive option, but pages often get ratty and fall out. I find that the best thing for me is a hardbound journal. These are good and sturdy and can be relatively inexpensive. Saving notes in an electronic format is the cleanest and most compact way to keep a notebook, but I like to have something that I can write on as I'm making the recipe so I don't leave anything out.

A good notebook will record the date each recipe was made and be set up in chronological order. That way, if something particularly valuable is learned and recorded with one recipe, it can be applied to later recipes, and there's a clear cutoff for which recipes it was applied to. This is also a helpful reminder of how old those bottles of soda are that are hiding in the back of the fridge or how old the roots are that were used in that last batch.

A page or two should be left blank at the beginning of the notebook to index it as needed. I like to write the name of the recipe, then record which page numbers it falls on. That way I know how many times I've made it and where to find each instance.

Eventually, the recipe will become solid and no more changes will need to be made. At that point, the final recipe becomes the standard for future batches.

If the recipe was made for someone else, it can be helpful to note that feedback as well. I have recipes that I think are good, but that some of my friends think are fantastic. It's easy to forget their reactions if I don't write them down. If I'm planning on making something for an event, I can tailor my recipe to the tastes of the people who will be there.

PRINCIPLES OF DEVELOPMENT

Recipe development is often a long process. Things rarely work out perfectly the first time. Some of my great recipes have often started out looking like dismal failures. If and when a new recipe fails, it's tempting to try to correct multiple things that didn't work out well. However, changing more than one component of a recipe at a time can skew results as to what worked well and what didn't. Was it the amount of vanilla that made it better or the amount of sugar? Did that bitterness come from steeping too much grain or from steeping it too hot? If more than one thing changed between batches, it may not be immediately clear what made the difference.

By changing one thing at a time, it builds experience as to what ingredients have a greater effect on the finished recipe than others. In addition to building a personal repertoire of recipes and ingredients, it also helps in analyzing other recipes. Just because a recipe pulled from the Internet contains a specific ingredient doesn't necessarily mean that it needs to be in there or that it can't be substituted with something else.

ADAPTING OTHER BEVERAGES

With the popularity of home carbonators such as the SodaStream, it's easy to turn a majority of beverages into homemade soda. Some of these may have mixed results. Powdered drink mixes can make good sodas with some careful preparation. It's best to make these into a thin syrup by adding just enough water to dissolve the sugars and flavors. This reduces the likelihood of losing carbonation to vigorous mixing. Some powdered mixes may contain aspartame, which breaks down with heating. When making a syrup with these mixes, it's important to keep any heating to a minimum.

Full-strength beverages such as juices or ready-to-drink teas can be carbonated under the right conditions. Fermentation is an easy option, though the flavor may change slightly. Force carbonation works very well for these given the right equipment.

I very much enjoy adapting recipes for other beverages, turning them into soda. A friend approached me once in hopes of creating a carbonated version

of a tea-free Russian tea recipe that his family made during the holidays. The recipe originally looked like this.

> Syrup:
> 2 cups (475 ml) water
> 2 cups (400 g) sugar
> Boil water with sugar for 5 minutes.
>
> Add:
> 2 cups (475 ml) orange juice
> ¾ cup (175 ml) lemon juice
> 2 teaspoons vanilla extract
> 2 teaspoons almond extract
> Bring to a boil and remove from heat.
>
> Add syrup to 2 quarts (1.9 L) water (hot or cold).

This would be an easy enough recipe to carbonate directly in a keg or siphon, and it would be a good candidate for a fermented recipe without any modification. For a syrup recipe to add to carbonated water, though, it needed some adjustment. The first thing was to separate as much water as I could to reserve for carbonated water later, including water from the orange juice by using a frozen juice concentrate.

> 2 cups (475 ml) water
> 2 cups (400 g) sugar
>
> ½ cup (120 ml) orange juice concentrate + 1½ cups (355 ml) water
> ¾ cup (175 ml) lemon juice
> 2 teaspoons vanilla extract
> 2 teaspoons almond extract
>
> 2 quarts water (64 ounces, or 1.8 L)
>
> Total water: 11½ cups (92 ounces, or 2.7 L)

I can bring the sugar to a boil with the lemon juice and then add the concentrate and let it cool. Once it has cooled, I can add the extracts. I don't want to boil the extracts with the syrup because they would partially boil off. So now my recipe looks like this.

> Syrup:
> 2 cups (400 g) sugar
> ¾ cup (175 ml) lemon juice
>
> Boil for 5 minutes, then add the following:
> ½ cup (120 ml) orange juice concentrate
> 2 teaspoons vanilla extract
> 2 teaspoons almond extract
>
> Add to 11½ cups (92 ounces, or 2.7 L) carbonated water.

The recipe here makes a little less than 1 gallon (128 ounces, or 3.6 L), which is my usual batch size. I like to scale my recipes to 1 gallon because it's a good reference for sweetener level, and it fits pretty well into the bottles that I have. I can easily squeeze an extra 0.8 ounce into a 12-ounce (355 ml) bottle,

so that comes out nicely to ten 12-ounce (355 ml) bottles or five 24-ounce (700 ml) bottles. I can also easily multiply it by 5 to make a full keg or divide by 4 if I want to do it in a 1-liter (¼ gallon) soda siphon. If I'm making a new recipe, I also like to compare syrup volume to water volume so I can adjust from there. Granulated sugar dissolves down to about half its dry volume, and all the other ingredients are liquid, so they're easy to calculate.

> 2 cups (400 g) sugar = 8 fluid ounces dissolved, or 235 ml
> ¾ cup lemon juice = 6 ounces, or 175 ml
> ½ cup orange juice concentrate = 4 ounces, or 120 ml
> 2 teaspoons vanilla extract = 0.33 ounce, or 10 ml
> 2 teaspoons almond extract = 0.33 ounce, or 10 ml
> Total syrup: 18.66 ounces (550 ml)
> Total water: 11½ cups (92 ounces, or 2.7 L)

$92 \div 18.66 = 4.93$. For ease of use, I'll say this is pretty close to a 5:1 ratio of water to syrup. This won't scale cleanly, so I know I'll need to make some adjustments that may affect flavor if I want a recipe that's easily scalable. I'm going to adjust the syrup recipe by increasing everything by about one-eighth of what's already there.

> 2¼ cups (450 g) sugar = 9 fluid ounces dissolved, or 250 ml
> ¾ cup + 2 tablespoons lemon juice = 7 ounces (200 ml)
> ½ cup + 1 tablespoon orange juice concentrate = 4½ ounces (135 ml)
> 2¼ teaspoons vanilla extract = 0.37 ounce = 11 ml
> 2¼ teaspoons almond extract = 0.37 ounce = 11 ml
> Total syrup: 21.24 ounces (607 ml)
> Total water: 13½ cups (108 ounces, or 3.2 L)

And there's the converted recipe, which makes a really, really tasty soda. We were all very pleased with how it turned out, and I get requests to remake it almost every time it runs out.

KNOW YOUR ROOTS

Understanding soda's roots both literally and figuratively is a necessary responsibility when using natural ingredients. In quite the contrast from today, sodas were originally used and marketed as healthful tonics to invigorate the body. The roots and herbs used to flavor them were not chosen simply for their flavor, but also for their therapeutic benefits. For instance, sassafras is known to have analgesic and antiseptic properties and was historically used for treatment of sexually transmitted diseases. Sarsaparilla was once used as an anti-inflammatory and aphrodisiac. Birch bark and oils contain some chemicals that are anti-inflammatory and others that are precursors to aspirin.

Some herbs and roots are widely used as folk remedies with only anecdotal evidence of their efficacy, whereas some are confirmed to contain compounds with documented medicinal effects. The upside is that it increases their availability. Look for dried herbs and roots in health food stores where bulk tea ingredients are sold. The downside is that homemade sodas using natural ingredients may have unintended side effects. Ginger and dandelion root can both be mild diuretics. Licorice root can sometimes contain a compound that elevates blood pressure and may cause complications for pregnant women or people with heart conditions. It's always best practice to research herbs and their uses before using them as flavoring ingredients.

Any ingredient that has a potent flavor usually has a potent aroma. Many herbs and roots with culinary and medicinal uses also find use in aromatherapy. Sometimes it's easy to find an extract or an essential oil that contains the flavor and aroma for this purpose; however, many of these are not food grade and may contain various solvent residues from the extraction process. When searching for oils to use as flavoring components, stick with essential oils and extracts that are specifically intended for food use. These are often sold as candy-making supplies.

Here is a quick rundown of most of the roots used in this book.

Sassafras root comes from the sassafras tree and has a strong aroma characteristic of root beer. The use of sassafras oil in foods was banned in 1960 by the FDA after studies linked it to cancer. Some speculation has also suggested that the ban also has something to do with safrole, an extract of sassafras, being a precursor to MDMA (Ecstasy) manufacture. Sassafras root is still available for sale in health food stores for use in teas because it qualifies as a dietary supplement. Its uses as a folk remedy include use as an anticoagulant.

Sarsaparilla root comes from certain species of the *Similax* genus, which are a group of climbing vines. The Mexican sarsaparilla has a number of folk remedies associated with it, including treatment for anemia and as a hormone booster. The Mexican variety is somewhat bitter, whereas the Indian variety, from an entirely different genus, has more of a vanilla characteristic.

Gentian root is ridiculously bitter. It is the primary component of Angostura Bitters and also lends its flavor to Maine's favorite soft drink, Moxie. It has been used as a remedy for high blood pressure and spasms. I have experienced its effects as a possible cure for loss of appetite. It seems that once it's on the tongue, the body and mind both crave something to replace the lingering and malevolent bitterness. Use it sparingly in recipes, if at all. I've included it in my Mockter Pepper recipe because it was an original ingredient in the Pepsin Bitters formula that surfaced a few years ago.

Ginger is used the world over as a flavor, aroma, and food component and for medicinal purposes. It has been used to reduce muscle pain and as a remedy for nausea. It has been used for relief of gastrointestinal problems, but it can have a negative effect on people with gallstones or ulcers.

Licorice root is one of the flavoring ingredients in traditional black licorice. It has a characteristic flavor similar to that of anise. It steeps well, and the flavors it brings out have a sweet taste in contrast to some of the other roots that come out with a bitter taste. It is used medicinally to treat ulcers and bowel disorders. It has numerous hormonal effects and can be toxic to the liver and heart and cause elevated blood pressure if consumed regularly or excessively.

Wild cherry bark can give a cherry taste and aroma, but it can also be a bit earthy. It is used sometimes for reducing inflammation and can have an astringent effect. Coupled together, those two properties make it common for use as a cough suppressant.

Dandelion root comes from the yellow flowering plant so common in much of the world. It is seen as a weed in many parts, but the entire plant is edible. It is used to treat infections by removing toxins from various parts of the body and as a diuretic. Some parts of the plant are high in potassium.

Burdock root comes from the plant that inspired Velcro. The root is chopped and eaten whole in some Asian countries. It contains tannins that render it somewhat bitter. As a remedy, it is also used as a diuretic.

Yucca root is sometimes confused with cassava root, but both have saponins, which will give a frothy head to any soda. Because of this property, it is said to have been used by Native Americans as a shampoo. It has also been used as a remedy for headaches and other maladies. Not all yucca species are edible, so be sure to check which species are suitable for use in soda.

COMPARING TO COMMERCIAL FLAVORS

Despite the endless variety of flavor possibilities with homemade soda, people still like to stick with what's tried and true. The flavors they grew up with still hold a magical nostalgia that people yearn for. While a discerning palate can pick out the distinct flavors in a ginger ale or a root beer, other flavors are more abstract, such as cola, the ever-popular Dr. Pepper, and the obscure Moxie. The flavoring components of these classic beverages may be a closely guarded secret, but the other ingredients are always disclosed. At first glance, it's surprising how much information can be gleaned from the label.

The first thing I look at is sugar level. Sugars are listed in grams under carbohydrates on the nutrition panel. To make up 1 pound, it takes 454 grams. A 12-ounce (355 ml) can of cola lists 39 g of sugar, and the serving size is the entire can. Assuming a 1-gallon batch (128 ounces, or 3.8 L), divide by 12 ounces and then multiply by 39 g.

128 ÷ 12 x 39 = 416 g sugar per gallon

Compare that to a root beer, which lists 32 g of sugar per 8-ounce (235 ml) serving:

128 ÷ 8 x 32 = 512 g sugar per gallon

If I'm making a cola, it will taste closer to the commercial version if I use less sugar per gallon than I normally like. If I'm making a root beer, it wouldn't taste out of place if I used a little more sugar than I usually use.

The next thing I look for on a label is what acids are used. The two most common are phosphoric acid and citric acid. Phosphoric acid is usually used in colas and sometimes root beer. It offers an almost dry, astringent flavor. Citric acid is used in just about everything else. It offers a bright, fresh, fruity flavor. The acid component, whichever it may be, balances with the carbonation and the sweetness for a well-rounded soda.

Other things on the ingredient panel give ideas on how it was made. Acacia gum is a common ingredient used for emulsifying flavor oils. It is often found in citrusy flavored sodas. Quillaia extract or yucca root extract are used for a frothier head and are sometimes found in root beers.

Top from left: gentian root (A), star anise (B), sarsaparilla root (C), ginger root (D), sassafras root (E), fresh dandelion roots (F), licorice root (G) (both with greens), burdock root (H), fresh yucca root (I).

three
SERVING SODA

As more and more friends and family started asking for some of my homemade sodas, it became apparent that I would rarely have to make any other type of food for a party or get-together ever again. In some cases, it is just assumed now that I'm supplying the drinks. With that said, it also soon became apparent that preparing homemade soda to serve to large groups could become tedious if the only thing to serve it in is 12-ounce (355 ml) glass bottles.

Luckily, there are other options, depending on how much of an investment in equipment is warranted for the occasion at hand. For entertaining at home, commercial postmix and even vintage premix systems are impressive options that can be purchased new or secondhand from restaurant equipment suppliers. However, they're not very portable, they can require some expertise to set up, and they can be pricey.

Just as many beer home brewers find kegging to be much less tedious than bottling, kegging soda is a viable option when serving for large groups. In fact, the used "home-brew kegs" (also called "corny kegs" for the Cornelius brand name) sold for beer making were once in distribution as soda fountain premix tanks. These can be used as originally intended with a premix system setup, or they can be used with beer dispensing equipment, which is usually readily available through many home-brew supply shops. Soda can just as well be carbonated in the larger, commercial-size Sanke kegs, though they are not as easy to fill and clean due to the smaller opening. When carbonating in kegs, a simple kegerator or draft box setup can be purchased or built, usually for much less than commercial equipment. Indeed, for most this is the preferred choice, as most of the equipment for doing so is more widely available.

POST-MIX

Post-mix setups are the most common form of fountain drink machine there is in use today. The syrup and carbonated water in these machines is mixed in the nozzle, or after carbonation, as the name implies. They need a power source, a constant water source, and a CO_2 source.

Their operation can seem very complicated but can be understood generally by getting to know the parts needed to make up a complete system. The first piece is the CO_2 tank and regulator. This feeds into the carbonator to supply a source of carbonation and also powers the syrup pumps. The carbonator is a pressure vessel with a constant water inlet fed by a pump to overcome the 100 psi operating pressure. This high pressure carbonates the water quickly and supplies an almost continuous supply of carbonated water to the nozzle. The nozzle is also fed by the aforementioned syrup pumps, which take syrup from a bag-in-box setup.

Using these setups for homemade soda can be tricky, but it's not out of the question. For those with enough dedicated space and the proper hookups, these can be set up to use homemade syrups instead of the commercial bag-in-box syrups.

SODAMAKING FAQ

Many homebrewers find that dispensing soda out of their draft beer equipment is less effective. Higher pressures and short beverage lines make the experience somewhat akin to getting a drink from a fire hose, leaving little carbonation. One very nice feature of an existing pre-mix system is the pressure compensation that already exists in the faucet. While draft beer faucets are inexpensive and easy to find, premix faucets can make the experience of serving soda a bit more bearable.

Premix tanks can be filled with syrup, pressurized, and included in the system without the need for syrup pumps.

The most common place to purchase these is from companies that liquidate restaurant equipment. Occasionally, smaller units can be picked up at a reasonable price, but a complete used setup can easily run $500 or more.

PREMIX

Premix systems were the standard for fountain drinks for many years before the post-mix systems were in such wide use. They are still in limited use today in venues such as fairgrounds or concessions trailers where a water line is not available to feed a carbonator.

The setup is much simpler than the post-mix and relies only on CO_2 pressure to operate. A ready-to-drink, carbonated beverage is hooked to the CO_2 regulator, which applies pressure that will then push it through the faucet. These systems are more difficult to find used, and typically any used premix equipment will have significantly more age on it than post-mix systems. Many are portable self-contained units that either have a refrigerated cold plate to cool the soda as it goes from the tank to the faucet or a cold plate under an ice bin.

Use of these systems for homemade soda is relatively simple because the premix tanks that they were designed to use are the same tanks that are available through home-brew supply shops and the adaptation is more or less just "plug and play" depending on the pin lock or ball lock configuration.

SODA SIPHONS AND OTHER COUNTERTOP CARBONATORS

The classic soda siphon was more or less the original way of carbonating soda in the home without the use of yeast. It has stood the test of time, and modern versions have changed little over the decades save for the materials they are made from. Original wire-mesh–encased glass bottled versions have mostly given way to the sturdier stainless steel or aluminum bottles, but the former can still be found on occasion. These can be used to carbonate anything liquid, provided they are adequately cleaned between uses. Serving soda from these can be tricky given that there's no pressure adjustment, but they can be a classy way to serve a small amount of beverage for entertaining. The single best piece of advice to get the best results when using one of these is simply to keep everything as cold as possible. Chill the filled siphon before charging and give it a good shake after it is charged. Let it chill a little bit more before serving so the pressure and carbonation have a chance to equilibrate.

Most home-brew supply stores that sell kegging setups will also have in stock a Carbonator cap. This is a plastic cap that fits most 2-liter (½ gallon) soda bottles and has a ball lock connector on top to hook up to a regulator. All that is required is to connect the CO_2 and shake until fully carbonated. Follow the same procedure as for soda siphons for the best results. This can be very handy for quick test batches with the option of having full control over carbonation pressure. Many people who don't want much investment past a CO_2 tank and regulator will go this route for quick, easy, and inexpensive home carbonating.

Much excitement and marketing has gone into the SodaStream in the past couple of years as a low cost, eco-friendly alternative to buying commercial soda. While there are lower-cost options, the SodaStream is indeed quite convenient. Its compact size fits on the countertop and hides the CO_2 tank

inside. This is, in a sense, the siphon reimagined. Anyone who has visited a big box store will likely be familiar with its looks if not its design. Instead of using chargers, it uses proprietary CO_2 refills that quite resemble in shape and function odd-size paintball tanks. Instead of serving from a siphon tube, the intention is to carbonate only water in a removable bottle to which syrups are later added. All of the recipes in this book are adapted for a seltzer-plus-syrup approach, and as such all of them are SodaStream friendly. Many of the SodaStream's critics cite the warranty's mandate that only water be carbonated in the device and the relatively high cost of the CO_2 refill exchanges as the product's biggest downfalls. Again, the best results here are obtained by keeping the water as cold as possible. The entire device need not be chilled, but keeping a filled bottle in the fridge until it's ready to be carbonated is a good idea.

With the SodaStream's success there have been a number of knockoffs. Some of them are also designed to carbonate water, while others can be used to carbonate just about anything. When deciding which is the best option, always consider ease of use, availability, and cost of CO_2 refills and the intended finished beverage. The principles for achieving the best results remain more or less the same. Keep everything chilled and don't overfill the bottles, and everything should be fine.

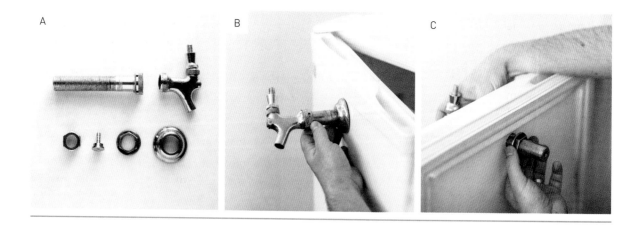

A   B   C

KEGERATOR

For those who aren't interested in scouring used equipment sales or auction sites waiting for the perfect piece to come along, or those who simply don't have the space to dedicate to the use of commercial soda-dispensing equipment but want to carbonate something more than a liter at a time, a home kegerator is another option that can be explored. Commercial versions are designed to be used with larger 15½-gallon (59 L) beer kegs, but they can be adapted for use with the smaller 5-gallon (19 L) premix soda tanks without much trouble. The Sanke adapter for the larger keg can be swapped for a pair of ball or pin lock connectors. One thing to take note of is the faucet. The faucet and fittings (including the shank, flange, lock nut, barbed tailpiece, and shank nut) are necessary additions in place of a picnic tap for use in a kegerator (A). Many dispensing systems used for beer will have a chrome-plated brass faucet, and while this will work for a short period of time, the chrome eventually wears off and exposes the brass underneath, which is susceptible to leaching from the carbonic and citric acids in soda. For peace of mind and durability, it's best to replace any chromed copper components that will come into contact with beverage (usually consisting of the tailpiece, the shank, and the faucet) with identical stainless steel parts.

Since a home kegerator is very similar in size and function to a typical mini fridge, it can sometimes be more practical to convert a mini fridge to a kegerator rather than purchasing one brand-new. Converting any fridge can be as simple as mounting a faucet in the door and connecting a beverage line (B). The faucet attaches to a shank and is fitted through the flange and then through the hole in the door (C). A lock nut holds the shank securely in the door and it is ready to connect the barbed tailpiece and hose.

A 3- to 4-cubic-foot (.9- to 1.2-cubic-meter) model will usually hold one soda keg, whereas to fit two kegs requires 4½ to 5 cubic feet (1.4 to 1.5 cubic meters). The best options for converting are those that don't have the evaporator at the top as a freezer section. Models that don't are difficult to come by, so many home brewers make do by carefully bending the U-shaped evaporator/freezer down and to the rear of the fridge to allow space for the tops of the kegs. Doing so is risky business, though, as a kink in the evaporator lines can cause leaks where the refrigerant can escape, rendering the fridge useless. A mistake like this is usually more costly to repair than replacing the entire fridge.

If more than one or two kegs need to be on tap at a time, a full-size fridge or chest freezer can also be converted. Full-size fridges are easy to come by as used appliances and simple to convert. Converted chest freezers (sometimes called "keezers") that are adjusted to hold temperatures above freezing are more efficient, but they can be a challenge if lifting a full keg into or out of it is going to be a daunting task.

RESOURCES

A full tutorial on converting appliances is a bit beyond the scope of this book, but there are many who have documented their own conversions to share their experiences with others. For those who choose to repurpose a used appliance or void the warranty on a new one, countless design ideas and build tutorials are readily available online in various places. Home-brew forums and clubs are great resources for help with things like this. If there's anything that the home-brewing community does well other than brewing beer, it's fostering open collaboration and creative DIY attitudes. Home kegerator build tutorials run the gamut from contraptions that look like they were created by Dr. Frankenstein to classy pieces of furniture that bring plenty of form to the function.

HOME-BREW FORUMS

There are a handful of very helpful online forums that are dedicated to home brewing. With all the members' combined years of experience in home beverage making (alcoholic or not), forums are probably the single most important resource available for soda making. Because home-brewed beer and homemade soda share a significant amount of equipment and technique, lots of information available for one can be applied to the other. Many forum members dabble in both arenas and are glad to offer help even to those with no interest in beer brewing or even beer at all. They'll offer help on anything from kegerator building to recipe advice. Home Brew Talk and Northern Brewer are

probably the two biggest forums, the former with a fairly active soda subforum. Beer Advocate and the American Homebrewers Association also have active and popular forums, but with less in the soda category. See the Resources section on page 148 for more information.

HOME-BREW SHOPS

Most larger cities have a decent home-brew supply or wine-making shop. While almost anything from equipment to ingredients can be found readily on the Internet, I'm a big fan of buying local. Prices may be higher at the brick and mortar store, but not having to pay shipping on a bag of bottle caps or a packet of yeast is a pretty sizeable advantage. And while they are set up to make a profit, I've yet to see a store that is not owned and operated by anything less than an enthusiastic hobbyist, happy to help and share experiences with others. They're usually happy to field questions from anyone who needs help with a recipe or piece of equipment.

INDUSTRIAL SUPPLIERS

It's important to remember that most of the equipment for home kegging was designed to be used in a commercial food service setting, so sometimes the best source for parts or equipment can be an industrial supplier. The biggest supplier of beverage systems is the CHI Company, which carries a number of beer- and soda-serving options, including new and used equipment along with tools, minor parts, and hoses for upkeep and maintenance. They are one of the only places where I've seen brand-new premix tanks that are intended for soda rather than those sold through home-brew supply stores. When picking up any used premix or post-mix systems from any source that has not refurbished it, CHI is a great place to look for repair or replacement parts before taking on a DIY refurbishing project.

Micro Matic is another industrial supplier that sells direct to consumers and deals mostly with kegged beer dispensing. They sell everything from

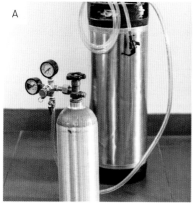

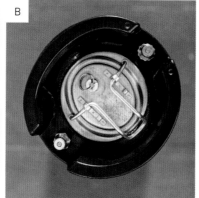

complete kegerators to kits to individual components. They even have a forum that's dedicated to draft system topics for both commercial and private systems. For anyone who really wants to learn all the ins and outs of kegging and serving, Micro Matic is essentially a one-stop shop.

KEGGING OVERVIEW

After having browsed the home-brew forums and suppliers regularly for quite some time, I see a lot of the same questions come up with regard to kegging time and time again. For anyone who's unfamiliar with the setup, it can be daunting to fully understand what's needed and what's not. It would be difficult to address them one by one, but a solid overview should cover the answers to most of the common questions.

GETTING KEGS AND THE EQUIPMENT

Some of the best places for acquiring kegging equipment are the online home-brew retailers. They usually have much larger selection and inventory available than smaller local shops, and many of them run promotions and deals for free shipping from time to time. Sometimes premix tanks can be purchased direct from a bottler that is looking to retire a few, but this is becoming less and less

common. Many are used anyway, so classified ads and online auction sites are as good a place as any to find people selling home-brew kegs, sometimes at really low prices.

After acquiring some used kegs, it's often immediately evident that they've likely seen better days. This is common, as some may have been in service for upward of 20 to 30 years. The first thing to do is get to know what's what and understand how to keep them in working order.

THE COMPLETE SYSTEM

The operation of a home-brew keg system **(A)** is not as complicated as it first looks. The top of the keg basically contains all the removable and working parts of a ball lock **(B)** or pin lock keg. The references here are for ball lock kegs and parts, but those on pin lock kegs are usually identical save for the posts and the absence of a manual relief valve. To distinguish the gas post from the liquid post, there are grooves cut parallel to the base of the post. Wrench and thread sizes can vary among manufacturers, but O-ring sizes are standard, as they are the most commonly replaced parts.

The lid fits down inside the keg and pressure seals it against the top. In order to remove the lid, the keg must be depressurized first. Most ball lock lids have a ring-pull pressure relief valve, whereas the pressure valve in many pin lock kegs is a passive safety valve that will only release at a certain pressure. The lids are interchangeable between pin and ball locks, so it's not uncommon to find one with the other type of lid.

The posts are essentially a type of pin valve where the center poppet is depressed to open the valve. The liquid post and the gas post on ball lock kegs are sized slightly differently to discourage mixing up the disconnects, though it still happens on occasion. The posts on pin lock kegs have different pin arrangements, so mixing up the disconnects is virtually impossible. The gas side disconnect is usually gray, while the liquid side is usually black. Underneath the posts, which twist off of the threaded terminal, are the dip tubes. A 2-inch (5 cm) tube is for the incoming gas, and a longer tube that reaches to the bottom is for the outgoing liquid. The operation is simple. As gas goes in, it pushes liquid out.

The process of carbonation is simply pressurizing the keg with liquid inside and allowing the water to absorb the CO_2. The CO_2 must be regulated down to a more manageable 20 to 35 psi from the 600 to 800 psi or more in the tank (C). The corny kegs are rated up to 130 psi, but most regulators that are designed for use in beer systems will have safety valves that release at 55 to 60 psi, which is more than adequate for soda making.

Most kegging kits sold through home-brew stores come with about a 5-foot (1.5 meter) length of beverage line hooked up to a picnic tap. While this length of line is adequate for beer, which is less carbonated, it is rather short for dispensing soda. A longer length of line will add more resistance to flow, which reduces the force of the soda at the tap. This is one common problem that many home-brewers face when making soda. While the soda may be properly carbonated in the keg, it will lose quite a bit of that if it is too forcefully dispensed.

Many recommendations based on various pressures put the proper length of serving line anywhere between 15 and 30 feet (4.6 to 9 meters). When purchasing a system specifically for soda, it would be worthwhile to upgrade to a longer line, though it can be quite cumbersome.

Regarding picnic taps: These are inexpensive plastic and are not built to very exacting standards. Some are sturdier than others. Sometimes the pressure of carbonating a beverage can cause the taps to leak, so it is a good idea to keep them disconnected when not serving so that an entire keg is not lost unknowingly.

TESTING THE EQUIPMENT

Once all the components are put together, it's important to be sure everything is in working order. First, be sure to check that all the connections are secure and tight. It's recommended to secure the CO_2 tank so that it doesn't tip over and damage the regulator or break the valve. A fire extinguisher holder works well, or even a simple Velcro strap can get the job done.

When opening the valve on the tank, the high pressure gauge at the end of the regulator should read around 800, depending on the temperature of the tank. Then twisting the regulator knob or screw will register on the low pressure gauge above. Usually this will read the output pressure of the regulator, not necessarily the pressure in the keg. When hooked up to the keg, there will be an audible hiss or squeal as the keg pressurizes. This will slowly die down as the pressure equilibrates, but if hissing continues for longer than a few minutes, then there is likely a leak somewhere in the system.

The faucet or tap should be hooked up to be sure that there is no blockage in the line. This can happen sometimes when using a juice with excessive pulp, or if syrup has not been properly mixed in. If liquid flows freely from the faucet and there are no leaks, then everything is working smoothly.

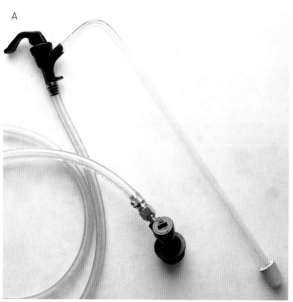

TIPS FOR BEST RESULTS

Sometimes people get into kegging and are underwhelmed by the quality of the beverage or frustrated by the experience. Sometimes it is not carbonated enough, they have some concerns about the equipment, or they find it more difficult than expected. It doesn't have to be this way. With a few tips, the experience can be much more straightforward and enjoyable.

Pressure It's important to remember that adequate pressure and proper carbonation are both related to temperature. Pressure will change with temperature regardless of where the regulator is set. A DIY kegerator can be set up with the CO_2 tank either inside the refrigerator compartment or outside it. When adjusting the regulator, in order to get consistent pressure output, it is important to set it at the temperature at which the tank and regulator will normally operate. If it is to be stored inside the fridge, let it chill before setting the proper pressure.

Time Many people don't get adequate carbonation because they don't wait until the liquid in the keg has been fully saturated with CO_2. Using a carbonation cap on a 2-liter (½ gallon) bottle, a soda siphon, or

countertop carbonater machine can yield almost instantaneous results. This is not necessarily the case when carbonating a larger volume in a keg. The rate at which this happens is not linear. As mentioned before, the hiss or squeal of the regulator is quite audible at first, but it tapers off quickly. Even after this point, the liquid is still slowly absorbing CO_2. The time it takes for the keg to fully reach equilibrium and be fully carbonated will vary based on temperature, agitation, and other solutes. Setting the pressure at the desired level and then shaking vigorously will hasten the process. When the needle on the regulator gauge no longer jumps as the keg is shaken, it is nearly fully carbonated. Give it another few hours after this point for proper carbonation.

Temperature Because gas solubility increases as temperature decreases, liquids will carbonate faster and more fully when they are colder. If there's not enough refrigerator space to pre-chill a keg, substituting some of the water in a kegged recipe with ice is one of the quickest ways to get the most carbonation into a keg. With shaking and ice, I've been able to get a keg of water adequately carbonated for addition to syrups in as little as an hour.

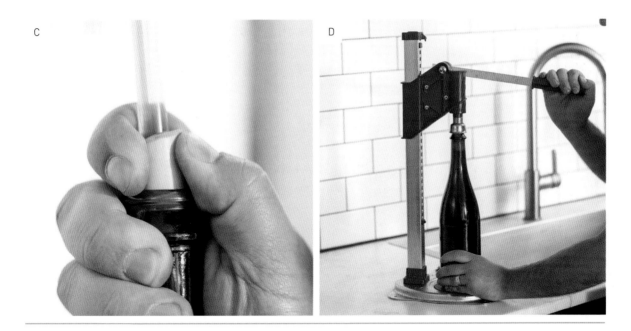

Bottling from the Keg For portability and variety, sometimes it's easier and more fun to have soda in bottles. A surefire way to keep optimal carbonation in a beverage when filling from a keg to a bottle is to use a counterpressure filler. A basic counterpressure filler can be as simple as a length of rigid tubing through a drilled rubber stopper **(A)**. The tubing slips into the picnic tap and the stopper seals the top of the bottle. The idea is to let the pressure build in the bottle **(B)** in order to slow the flow from the keg and keep as much carbonation as possible in the beverage. When it has settled somewhat in the bottle, pressure is gently released **(C)** by easing up on the stopper so that the change in pressure is not so sudden and violent as to to knock a lot of CO_2 out of solution. After releasing all of the pressure, the bottle can be capped **(D)**.

A true counterpressure filler will hook a separate line to the CO_2 source to purge the bottle of oxygen first. This is important for beer so that it will not oxidize and skunk, but for soda the only purpose it serves is to slow the flow from the faucet from the very beginning of the fill rather than letting the pressure build simply from displacement of the beverage. This is especially helpful with very foamy beverages as it keeps them from foaming too quickly.

Serving from the Keg Whether serving from a picnic tap or from a draft faucet designed for beer, the serving line should be long enough to offer resistance nearly equal to the pressure in the keg. Serving soda works well with a smaller inside diameter beverage line such as 3/16 inch (5 mm) or even as small as 1/8 inch (3 mm). Resistance from these lines is estimated to be between 2 and 3 psi per foot (30.5 cm) for 3/16-inch (5 mm) line and 5 to 8 psi per foot (30.5 cm) for 1/8-inch (3 mm) line. When building a system, the pressure and serving lengths should be balanced to be able to serve without losing a lot of carbonation. Multiplying the length of the line by the resistance per foot should give a total psi slightly less than the total pressure on the keg. If the resistance of the length of the line from the keg to the serving area turns out to be greater than the pressure on the keg, switch to a larger diameter line instead of increasing the pressure.

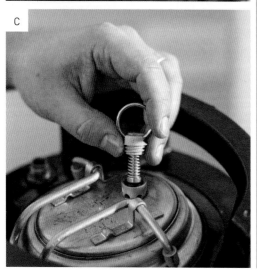

BASIC TROUBLESHOOTING AND MAINTENANCE

When something goes wrong or the outcome isn't as expected, understanding the function of all the parts makes identifying the problem much easier. Mostly it boils down either to not having enough pressure or to having too much. Not enough pressure either keeps the soda from flowing from the keg or keeps it from carbonating fully and can be caused by a faulty regulator, a blockage in the line, or nearly empty CO_2 tank. Too much pressure causes excessive foaming with little retained carbonation out of the tap and it can also cause leaks around the pressure relief valves. The most common problem otherwise is CO_2 leaks that stem from deteriorated O-rings or fittings that are not tightened down correctly. Keeping a keg well maintained can prevent some of these things.

Teardown and Cleaning Most kegs that look dilapidated are merely in need of a good cleaning. Depending on how long the keg has sat unused, this could seem a daunting task. Cola of unknown age is often not a pretty sight. For a deep cleaning, more than just the lid will need to be removed.

After removing the lid, remove the posts. **(A)** Removing posts is simply a matter of finding the right wrench. A hex head post can be removed with a box or crescent wrench. Some kegs have one post that has a twelve-point star and requires a deep wall socket. A socket makes removal much easier, but with multiple kegs there can be a variety of wrench sizes required. Pin lock posts require a slotted socket that will fit over the pins.

Once the posts have been removed, the dip tubes should slide out after some gentle coaxing. **(B)** If the keg has been sitting for a while with old soda or syrup in it, then these will require more than just soapy water and sanitizer to clean properly. A dip tube brush is the easiest solution for getting the grime out.

When cleaning, take time to inspect for any rust spots, cracks, or other areas of concern. The threaded terminals where the posts attach can be particularly grimy and should come clean with a stainless steel-friendly powdered cleanser such as

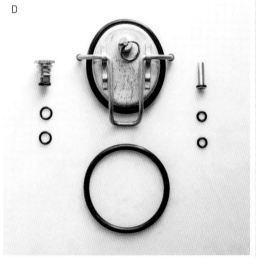

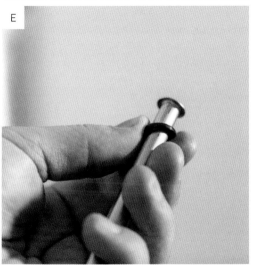

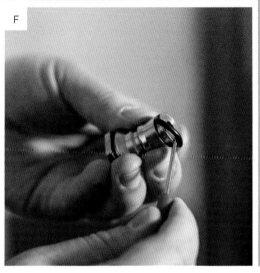

Bar Keepers Friend. Relief valves need to be changed occasionally **(C)**, but not as often as O-rings. Be careful to avoid damaging the plastic threads.

For sanitizing, use a sanitizer that is safe for stainless steel. Any bleach-based sanitizers will cause pits that can harbor bacteria or cause leaks around the seals. There are acid-based and iodophor sanitizers that are effective and safe for stainless steel and are available at most home-brew or wine-making shops.

O-Ring Replacement The O-rings are easily replaceable and with luck the only maintenance that needs to be done on a used keg. **(D)** O-rings should be replaced if they are misshapen, have an odor, or show other signs of wear or deterioration. Home brewers of both beer and soda will typically dedicate kegs for soda because the O-rings and rubber seals on the poppets tend to absorb the strong flavors of sodas such as root beer and cola. It would be advisable to replace the O-rings of a recently acquired used keg when its history is uncertain.

First, remove the old O-rings. O-rings from the tubes are easy enough to slide off. **(E)** Post O-rings may require a pick to stretch up and off the post. **(F)** Try to avoid scratching the stainless steel posts with steel that is non-stainless, as scratches will promote pitting and rusting.

Give new O-rings a good rinse to remove any manufacturing oils or dust. When reassembling everything, it never hurts to soak everything in sanitizer to be safe, posts and poppets included.

Reassembly is simply the reverse of disassembly, though take care not to switch the in and out posts or dip tubes. A silicone-based lubricant designed for faucet repair may be used on a keg that has difficulty sealing, but is not always necessary. This can be found at nearly any hardware store and is usually beneficial for difficult-to-seal lids and to make the disconnects easier to get on and off of the posts. If everything went together smoothly, and nothing cross threaded, there's no need to go excessively tight. Overtightening can weaken the post terminals and cause pinhole leaks, which pretty much doom the keg to the scrap yard.

Checking for Leaks Once everything is back together, it's time to pressurize the keg and test the new seals. To use less CO_2 while pressurizing, fill the keg with water. I like to go up to 30 to 35 psi, as that seals the lid quite well, and that's usually the pressure used to carbonate a soda. Hissing is a definite indicator of leaking, but a slow leak may not be audible. To find slower leaks or if a hissing leak is difficult to pinpoint, spray the lid with soapy water. **(A)** Bubbles will be visible right away from the spray, but watch for the formation of new bubbles or watch for movement of existing ones. A steady leak will usually create numerous uniform bubbles. **(B)**

After replacing the O-rings, if there is a leak from the dip tube or lid, it can sometimes be fixed by depressurizing and adjusting the valves to get it seated correctly. I find that most of my leaks occur from places that just need some slight adjustment such as tightening the post or relief valve or reseating the lid. The relief valves and poppets do need to be changed on occasion, but not as regularly as O-rings.

If a leak cannot be stopped with part replacement, reseating or tightening the lid or dip tube, and application of lubricant, then it may be time to retire

SODAMAKING FAQ

Leaks can be pervasive and expensive if not found and remedied. What can be done if a leak can't be located, yet CO_2 is still being lost? I've found the best practice to deal with leaks is to turn off the valve on the CO_2 tank when it is not in use. If the rush of CO_2 is audible when turning the valve back on after long periods between use, there's likely a leak in the system. Check all the connections between the keg and the tank regularly. If that doesn't work, submerging a pressurized keg in a full bathtub and looking for bubbles can sometimes be effective. While some connections can also be submerged, the regulator and gauges are best left out of the water.

the keg. That may mean finding a homebrewer who needs an extra keg for fermentation or sanitizer storage, or it may mean a trip to the scrapyard.

CONVERTING OR ADDING TO AN EXISTING WET BAR

The perfect dedicated space in a home for dispensing equipment is a wet bar. Whether it be a simple backbar countertop with a sink against the wall in the basement or a walk-behind bar, there is usually ample space to put in at least something. There are a few guidelines to keep in mind other than what has already been discussed.

When choosing equipment, consider the space, electrical, and water resources available. Post-mix systems always require all three. Premix systems usually only take up space and will only require electricity if the system is refrigerated.

For a kegerator or a converted mini fridge or freezer, it looks really nice to have just a tap tower on the bar with the refrigerator tucked out of sight, but there are a couple of problems with doing so. The first is that any length of line running outside of the fridge will hold warm soda if it sits for too long. This not only causes excessive foaming for the first pour out of the faucet but also creates the possibility of microbial growth in the line over time. If the tower or faucet is not to be directly attached to the refrigerator, one solution would be splicing in or setting up an extra CO_2 or water line in order to purge or flush the section that sits unrefrigerated. Another solution, albeit a more expensive one, is to install a glycol cooling system with your lines. These are commonly used in large keg dispensing operations to keep the lines of beverage from getting too warm if they are to travel very far. Usually the cold glycol line is run with any other lines surrounding it and insulated. This bundle of tubing or "trunk line" will keep the beverage lines cold over long distances but requires a circulating reservoir of refrigerated glycol, which can be pricey.

Another consideration with a converted mini fridge is placement. Most modern mini fridges

dissipate heat through the metal skin on the sides and top, where the condenser coils are mounted just under the surface. Because of this design, they usually require some clearance on these sides to function properly. Check with the manufacturer to determine if the fridge is rated for built-in installation. Converted freezers will have similar clearance requirements to dissipate heat properly. Many home brewers have built a converted freezer into a home bar without much clearance or have built a beautifully woodworked cabinet over it only to find that they've reduced the working life of the freezer to only a few short years.

Because different refrigerators and freezers have different condenser configurations, a little research before drilling holes for beverage and gas lines can prevent the embarrassment and devastation of turning it into a paperweight by nicking a condenser line. One way to avoid puncturing a line is to locate its general location from the outside by feeling for hot spots after the compressor has been running for a while. After a spot has been chosen for drilling a hole, first carefully drill a pilot hole from the inside. Then carefully chip away the insulation to the outer skin. Once enough insulation is removed, any condenser lines can be felt by prodding around with something that won't pierce any metal. When it is certain that there are no lines to puncture, then it is safe to complete the hole by drilling through the outside metal sheeting. The safest place to drill holes on any fridge is the doors. Many larger refrigerators that have condenser coils on the back or underneath will usually be safe for drilling through the sides as well.

four
RECIPES

In putting together recipes, I've tried to assemble a list that will present a wide range of options for the beginner as well as the experienced. Some are basic recipes to build a familiarity with ingredients and flavors, while some are designed to teach technique, but all are meant to be thoroughly enjoyed. Many are exclusive to this book, though there are some shining stars that have been carried over from my blog. Additionally, all are adapted to the three different soda-making methods so that they have a wider appeal. It can be frustrating to find a good-looking recipe only to discover that it requires special equipment or ingredients. Ingredients and technique are listed here, but more detailed recipe templates are found on pages 22, 25, and 27.

I've categorized these recipes based on their flavor types: Fruity, Root and Herbal Teas, and Indulgent, along with Experimental recipes with vegetables or bizarre origins, and since I've always felt that soda was meant to be a special treat rather than a regular staple, I've also included recipes for Holidays and Special Occasions.

These recipes are also meant to be adapted to individual tastes. I have found that those who are looking at homemade soda for health benefits often prefer to cut back on the sugar, and that those who are less fond of citrus flavors like to dial back the fruit juices a bit. Don't feel obligated to follow the recipes to the letter. Experimentation is the best way to really master the soda-making craft.

fruity

This is one of my all-time favorite recipes. It's an easy one that packs in a lot of well-balanced flavor. It's a definite crowd-pleaser even for those who don't like lime or coconut separately. The coconut water on its own doesn't have enough flavor to balance out the acidity of the lime, but it makes the flavor more complex than just the coconut extract alone. Be careful with this recipe, though—the flavor imparts a strong desire to be sitting on the beach breathing in an island breeze. For a slightly more complex flavor, try using coconut sugar instead of granulated white sugar.

COCONUT LIME

In a saucepan, combine the sugar, 1 cup (235 ml) of the water, and 1 tablespoon (15 ml) of the lemon juice. Heat over medium-high heat until the sugar has dissolved and the syrup has boiled for about 5 minutes.

FOR THE SYRUP AND SELTZER METHOD Remove from the heat and chill. Add rest of the juices, the coconut water, and the extract and then add the syrup to carbonated water.

FOR STRAIGHT CARBONATION OR FERMENTATION Add the rest of the water, the juices, the coconut water, and the extract.

FOR STRAIGHT CARBONATION Chill the mixture before adding it to the keg or carbonator of your choice.

FOR FERMENTATION Hydrate the yeast in ¼ cup (60 ml) or less of warm water. Add the hydrated yeast to the mixture after it has cooled to 10 to 15°F (5.5 to 8°C) above room temperature. Stir in the yeast nutrient. Mix well and then bottle.

YIELD 1 GALLON (3.8 L)

RECIPE VARIANT

Use the zest from the limes for a more intense lime flavor without added sourness or substitute pineapple juice for the citrus to make a piña colada flavor soda.

SYRUP + SELTZER

2 cups (400 g) sugar

1 cup (235 ml) water

2 tablespoons (28 ml) fresh lemon juice

⅓ cup (80 ml) fresh lime juice

¾ cup (177 ml) coconut water without pulp

1 teaspoon coconut extract

(syrup for 1 gallon [3.8 L] finished soda; use 1½ to 2 tablespoons [25 to 28 ml] per 8 ounces [235 ml] carbonated water, or to taste)

STRAIGHT CARBONATION

2 cup sugar (400 g)

13¼ cups (3.1 L) water

2 tablespoons (28 ml) fresh lemon juice

⅓ cup (80 ml) fresh lime juice

¾ cup (177 ml) coconut water without pulp

1 teaspoon coconut extract

FERMENTATION

2¼ cups (450 g) sugar

12½ cups water (2.9 L)

2 tablespoons (28 ml) fresh lemon juice

½ cup (120 ml) fresh lime juice

1 cup (235 ml) coconut water without pulp

1¼ teaspoons coconut extract

⅛ teaspoon Champagne yeast

1 g yeast nutrient

Peach soda can sometimes be a little tricky to pull off. Too much fruit and sugar gives the impression of drinking the syrup straight from canned peaches, but too little and the flavor is weak and underwhelming. Added white grape juice really brings out the freshness of the peaches and mellows down the canned or cooked flavor. Rounding out the peach flavor with some vanilla would be another good way to find the spot between too harsh and too weak. Don't be tempted to leave the peach peels on for more color in the syrup; the fuzz makes them really difficult to clean very well, and the color impact is minimal at best.

PEACH

In a saucepan, combine the sugar and 1 cup (235 ml) of the water. Heat over medium-high heat until the sugar has dissolved and the syrup begins to boil. Remove the syrup from the heat and pour over the peaches to macerate. Using a potato masher, crush the macerated peaches to further release their juice. Using a fine-mesh strainer, strain the fruit pulp from the syrup as fully as possible. Add the juice concentrate to the strained syrup.

FOR THE SYRUP AND SELTZER METHOD Chill the syrup and add to carbonated water.

FOR STRAIGHT CARBONATION OR FERMENTATION Add the rest of the water to the strained syrup.

FOR STRAIGHT CARBONATION Chill the mixture before adding it to the keg or carbonator of your choice.

FOR FERMENTATION Hydrate the yeast in ¼ cup (60 ml) or less of warm water. Add the hydrated yeast to the mixture after it has cooled to 10 to 15°F (5.5 to 8°C) above room temperature. Stir in the yeast nutrient. Mix well and then bottle.

YIELD 1 GALLON (3.8 L)

TECHNIQUE
PEELING PEACHES

It's best to remove the skin from the peaches because the fuzz makes them difficult to clean. Blanching them to get the skin off can make short work of peeling, particularly when using a lot for a large batch.

1. Bring a medium-size pot of water to a boil. Prepare a bowl of ice water to plunge the peaches in after they're blanched.

2. Place the peaches in the boiling water to blanch for 30 seconds to 1 minute. **(A)**

3. Remove them from the boiling water and immediately place them in the ice water. Let them sit in the ice water for the same amount of time as they sat in the boiling water.

4. After removing from the ice water, the peels should more or less slide right off. **(B)** Peaches that aren't very ripe will be difficult to peel and some varieties just don't peel well at all. These may take extra time in the boiling water.

TECHNIQUE
MASHING FRUITS

With most fruits, letting the heat and sugar from a syrup break down the fruit will do part of the work of getting all the flavorful juices out.

1. Place the fruit in an empty saucepan or heat-proof bowl. Larger fruits should be diced, but most berries are fine as is.

2. In a saucepan, bring a sugar solution (simple syrup or invert syrup) to a boil. Remove from the heat and pour over the fruit, tossing to coat. **(A)**

3. After 10 to 15 minutes, use a potato masher to mash up what's left of the fruit. Riper fruit will break down more quickly than less-ripe fruit. **(B)**

4. Using a fine-mesh sieve, strain the syrup into a bowl. Toss the mash left in the sieve or gently press it to remove as much syrup as possible. A quick rinse will transfer some of the residual sugar and flavor to the bowl, but it will also thin the syrup. **(C)**

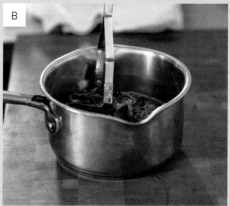

Strawberries are a big part of early summer. A summer picnic wouldn't be complete without fresh strawberries in pies, with short-cake, or as part of a fruit salad. Strawberry on its own is a classic soda flavor sure to evoke memories of a bygone era. Using the deepest red strawberries will give the soda the best color and flavor. If the soda comes out with a flat or cooked strawberry flavor, add a tablespoon or two of lemon juice to freshen it up a notch.

STRAWBERRY

In a saucepan, combine the sugar and 1 cup (235 ml) of the water. Heat on medium-high heat until the sugar has dissolved and the syrup begins to boil. Remove the syrup from the heat and pour over the berries to macerate. Using a potato masher, crush the macerated berries to further release the juice. Using a fine mesh strainer, strain the fruit pulp and seeds from the syrup as fully as possible.

FOR THE SYRUP AND SELTZER METHOD Chill the syrup and add to carbonated water.

FOR STRAIGHT CARBONATION OR FERMENTATION Add the rest of the water to the strained syrup.

FOR STRAIGHT CARBONATION Chill the mixture before adding it to the keg or carbonator of your choice.

FOR FERMENTATION Hydrate the yeast in ¼ cup (60 ml) or less of warm water. Add the hydrated yeast to the mixture after it has cooled to 10 to 15°F (5.5 to 8°C) above room temperature. Stir in the yeast nutrient. Mix well and then bottle.

YIELD 1 GALLON (3.8 L)

SYRUP + SELTZER

2 cups (400 g) sugar

1 cup (235 ml) water

2 cups whole strawberries (290 g, or about 20 medium berries)

(syrup for 1 gallon [3.8 L] finished soda; use 2 to 3½ tablespoons [28 to 55 ml] per 8 ounces [235 ml] carbonated water, or to taste)

STRAIGHT CARBONATION

2 cups (400 g) sugar

14 cups (3.3 L) water

2 cups whole strawberries (290 g, or about 20 medium berries)

FERMENTATION

2¼ cups (450 g) sugar

14 cups (3.3 L) water

2½ cups whole strawberries (363 g, or about 25 medium berries)

⅛ teaspoon Champagne yeast

1 g yeast nutrient

TECHNIQUE
ZESTING CITRUS

The zest of citrus fruits is the colored portion of the peel. This has pores that hold the strongly scented and flavored oil that gives citrus some of its astringency and appeal but doesn't have the bitterness of the white pith underneath. The best thing to use is a classic zester or a Microplane grater, but careful work with a knife will also work.

1. With a zester or Microplane, pulling off the zest from the peel is difficult to mess up. A scrubbing action will shave off the right amount of zest, but excessive passes over the same area will eventually dig into the pith. **(A)**

2. With a sharp knife, a shaving movement will usually yield the best results. If white spots show through, as seen here, it means the knife is cutting too deep. **(B)**

Lemon-lime is a classic soda flavor that has stood the test of time. It's a versatile beverage that can be used as a mixer or imbibed on its own. Adjusting the sugar a little lower will allow the citrus flavors to shine more and taste less syrupy. Though any commercial version is almost always a crystal-clear soda, this variant using natural juices and zest will have a little less clarity than the typical off-the-shelf version. The added freshness and burst of citrus flavor more than make up for the slightly cloudy look. If a crystal-clear look is a must, try using lemon and lime oils instead of zest and juice.

LEMON LIME

In a saucepan, combine the zests and water. For the syrup and seltzer method, use 1 cup (235 ml) water; otherwise, use as much water as is practical to strain. Bring to a boil and then remove from the heat and let steep for 20 minutes. Strain out the zest and return the water to the saucepan. Add the sugar and 1 tablespoon (15 ml) of the juice and bring to a boil over medium-high heat. Let boil for about 5 minutes. Remove the syrup from the heat and add the rest of the juices.

FOR THE SYRUP AND SELTZER METHOD Chill the syrup and add to carbonated water.

FOR STRAIGHT CARBONATION OR FERMENTATION Add the rest of the water to the strained syrup.

FOR STRAIGHT CARBONATION Chill the mixture before adding it to the keg or carbonator of your choice.

FOR FERMENTATION Hydrate the yeast in ¼ cup (60 ml) or less of warm water. Add the hydrated yeast to the mixture after it has cooled to 10 to 15°F (5.5 to 8°C) above room temperature. Stir in the yeast nutrient. Mix well and then bottle.

YIELD 1 GALLON (3.8 L)

SYRUP + SELTZER

Zest and juice of 2 lemons

Zest and juice of 2 limes

1 cup (235 ml) water

2 cups (400 g) sugar

(syrup for 1 gallon [3.8 L] finished soda; use 1½ to 2 tablespoons [25 to 28 ml] per 8 ounces [235 ml] carbonated water, or to taste)

STRAIGHT CARBONATION

Zest and juice of 2 lemons

Zest and juice of 2 limes

15 cups (3.5 L) water

2 cups (400 g) sugar

FERMENTATION

Zest and juice of 2 lemons

Zest and juice of 2 limes

15 cups (3.5 L) water

2¼ cups (450 g) sugar

⅛ teaspoon Champagne yeast

1 g yeast nutrient

The Italian limonata *is essentially a sparkling lemonade, but with more juice and tartness than Americans are accustomed to in a soda. These are becoming increasingly easier to find in the international section of supermarkets. It contains a fair amount of lemon juice, which gives it a robust, fresh lemon flavor. The lemon flavor is so robust that when using freshly squeezed lemon juice, the zest won't be missed if it's not used. Try the recipe as an uncarbonated mix in an ice cream maker for a traditional Sicilian granita.*

LIMONATA

In a saucepan, combine the sugar, ½ cup (120 ml) of the water, and 1 tablespoon (15 ml) of the lemon juice. Heat over medium-high heat until the sugar has dissolved and the syrup has boiled for about 5 minutes.

FOR THE SYRUP AND SELTZER METHOD Remove from the heat and chill. Add the rest of the juice and then add the syrup to carbonated water.

FOR STRAIGHT CARBONATION OR FERMENTATION Add the rest of the water and the juice.

FOR STRAIGHT CARBONATION Chill the mixture before adding it to the keg or carbonator of your choice.

FOR FERMENTATION Hydrate the yeast in ¼ cup (60 ml) or less of warm water. Add the hydrated yeast to the mixture after it has cooled to 10 to 15°F (5.5 to 8°C) above room temperature. Stir in the yeast nutrient. Mix well and then bottle.

YIELD 1 GALLON (3.8 L)

RECIPE VARIANT

Aranciata (orangeade), *sanguinella* (blood orange), and *pompelmo* (grapefruit) are all variants and are equally refreshing. Substitute juice from any of those fruits in this recipe for a good, strong citrus soda.

SYRUP + SELTZER

2 cups (400 g) sugar

½ cup (120 ml) water

2 cups (475 ml) fresh lemon juice

(syrup for 1 gallon [3.8 L] finished soda; use 3 to 4 tablespoons [45 to 60 ml] per 8 ounces [235 ml] carbonated water, or to taste)

STRAIGHT CARBONATION

2 cups (400 g) sugar

13 cups (3.1 L) water

2 cups (475 ml) fresh lemon juice

FERMENTATION

2¼ cups (450 g) sugar

13 cups (3.1 L) water

2 cups (475 ml) fresh lemon juice

⅛ teaspoon Champagne yeast

1 g yeast nutrient

1¾ cups (375 g) sugar

1 cup (235 ml) grape juice concentrate

½ cup (120 ml) water

(syrup for 1 gallon [3.8 L] finished soda; use 2 to 3 tablespoons [28 to 45 ml] per 8 ounces [235 ml] carbonated water, or to taste)

STRAIGHT CARBONATION

1¾ cups (375 g) sugar

1 cup (235 ml) grape juice concentrate or 4 cups (950 ml) 100% grape juice

Water to top up to 1 gallon

FERMENTATION

2 cups (400 g) sugar

1 cup (235 ml) grape juice concentrate or 4 cups (950 ml) 100% grape juice

Water to top up to 1 gallon

⅛ teaspoon Champagne yeast or red wine yeast

1 g yeast nutrient

Grape soda is a classic flavor. It's one that has been done by just about every bottler, but if not done right, it can be a really disappointing flavor. To get a nice grape character, the best thing to use is real grape juice. For a straight carbonation or a fermentation, full-strength or freshly squeezed grape juice can be used. For a syrup-plus-seltzer soda, it would be wasting money and destroying flavor by boiling down grape juice to a syrup consistency. Use a frozen concentrate instead because that work has been done already and under much better controlled conditions to preserve flavor.

GRAPE

In a saucepan, combine the sugar and half of the grape juice concentrate or juice. If using the concentrate, also add an equal amount of water so the syrup doesn't burn. Heat over medium-high heat until the sugar has dissolved and the syrup has boiled for about 5 minutes.

FOR THE SYRUP AND SELTZER METHOD Remove from the heat and chill. Add the rest of the juice concentrate and then add the syrup to carbonated water.

FOR STRAIGHT CARBONATION OR FERMENTATION Add the rest of the water and the concentrate or juice.

FOR STRAIGHT CARBONATION Chill the mixture before adding it to the keg or carbonator of your choice.

FOR FERMENTATION Hydrate the yeast in ¼ cup (60 ml) or less of warm water. Add the hydrated yeast to the mixture after it has cooled to 10 to 15°F (5.5 to 8°C) above room temperature. Stir in the yeast nutrient. Mix well and then bottle.

YIELD 1 GALLON (3.8 L)

Commercial orange sodas are usually flavored using only orange oil or an artificial flavor. I find that using the zest will get that dry citrus flavor, but adding in some juice as well will give a nice, sweet-tart, well-rounded orange flavor that tastes fresh. Using more orange juice will bring this closer to an Italian aranciata, *sister to the* limonata *recipe on page 65. Avoid juice with much pulp, as it will be difficult to keep carbonated, especially if serving through a keg.*

ORANGE

In a saucepan, combine the water and zest. For the syrup and seltzer method, use 1 cup (235 ml) water; otherwise, use as much water as is practical to strain. Bring to a boil and then remove from the heat and let steep for 20 minutes. Strain out the zest and return the water to the saucepan. Add the sugar and 1 tablespoon (15 ml) of the juice concentrate and bring to a boil over medium-high heat. Let boil for about 5 minutes. Remove the syrup from the heat and add the rest of the juices.

FOR THE SYRUP AND SELTZER METHOD Chill the syrup and add to carbonated water.

FOR STRAIGHT CARBONATION OR FERMENTATION Add the rest of the water to the strained syrup.

FOR STRAIGHT CARBONATION Chill the mixture before adding it to the keg or carbonator of your choice.

FOR FERMENTATION Hydrate the yeast in ¼ cup (60 ml) or less of warm water. Add the hydrated yeast to the mixture after it has cooled to 10 to 15°F (5.5 to 8°C) above room temperature. Stir in the yeast nutrient. Mix well and then bottle.

YIELD 1 GALLON (3.8 L)

RECIPE VARIANT

Double the orange zest and decrease the orange juice while adding in 1 teaspoon of pure vanilla extract for an Orange Creamsicle soda.

This popular flavor has been tickling innards since the 1940s. Many people are surprised to find that the primary ingredient after water and sweetener is orange juice concentrate. The orange, blended with lemon and lime zest, gives it a citrusy flavor that is not tied heavily to any one of the three fruits in particular. My version is a bit juicier and tarter than the commercial version, and it lacks the caffeine content that has primed so many youth for today's energy drink market. Yes, some people do genuinely like it solely for the flavor.

CITRUS DEW

In a saucepan, combine the water and zest. For the syrup and seltzer method, use 1 cup (235 ml) water; otherwise, use as much water as is practical to strain. Bring to a boil and then remove from the heat and let steep for 20 minutes. Strain out the zest and return the water to the saucepan. Add the sugar and 1 tablespoon (15 ml) of the orange juice concentrate or ¼ cup (60 ml) of the orange juice and bring to a boil over medium-high heat. Let boil for about 5 minutes. Remove the syrup from the heat and add the rest of the concentrate and juices.

FOR THE SYRUP AND SELTZER METHOD Chill the syrup and add to carbonated water.

FOR STRAIGHT CARBONATION OR FERMENTATION Add the rest of the water to the syrup.

FOR STRAIGHT CARBONATION Chill the mixture before adding it to the keg or carbonator of your choice.

FOR FERMENTATION Hydrate the yeast in ¼ cup (60 ml) or less of warm water. Add the hydrated yeast to the mixture after it has cooled to 10 to 15°F (5.5 to 8°C) above room temperature. Stir in the yeast nutrient. Mix well and then bottle.

YIELD 1 GALLON (3.8 L)

SYRUP + SELTZER

1 cup (235 ml) water

Zest and juice of 1 lemon

Zest and juice of 1 lime

2 cups (400 g) sugar

3 tablespoons (45 ml) orange juice concentrate

(syrup for 1 gallon [3.8 L] finished soda; use 2 to 3 tablespoons [28 to 45 ml] per 8 ounces [235 ml] carbonated water, or to taste)

STRAIGHT CARBONATION

Water to top up to 1 gallon

Zest and juice of 1 lemon

Zest and juice of 1 lime

2 cups (400 g) sugar

3 tablespoons (45 ml) orange juice concentrate or ¾ cup (175 ml) 100% orange juice

FERMENTATION

Water to top up to 1 gallon

Zest and juice of 1 lemon

Zest and juice of 1 lime

2¼ cups (450 g) sugar

3 tablespoons (45 ml) orange juice concentrate or ¾ cup (175 ml) 100% orange juice

⅛ teaspoon Champagne yeast

1 g yeast nutrient

SYRUP + SELTZER

2 cups (400 g) sugar

1 cup (235 ml) water

1 cup whole strawberries (145 g, or about 10 medium berries)

1 cup (145 g) blueberries

(syrup for 1 gallon [3.8 L] finished soda; use 2½ to 4 tablespoons [40 to 60 ml] per 8 ounces [235 ml] carbonated water, or to taste)

STRAIGHT CARBONATION

2 cups (400 g) sugar

14 cups (3.3 L) water

1 cup whole strawberries (145 g, or about 10 medium berries)

1 cup (145 g) blueberries

FERMENTATION

2¼ cups (450 g) sugar

14 cups (3.3 L) water

1¼ cups whole strawberries (181 g, or about 12 medium berries)

1 cup (145 g) blueberries

⅛ teaspoon Champagne yeast

1 g yeast nutrient

Berry-flavored sodas are usually hit or miss. Sometimes they're great. Sometimes they're just kind of there, taking up space. Using fresh handpicked berries that are at their seasonal peak and keeping the heat as minimal as possible is by far the best way to approach this recipe. What's great, though, is how customizable the recipe is. Straight blueberries can be used, or mix as many berries as are available. I like an equal amount of strawberries and blueberries, mainly because they're the most abundant in my locale. If heating ends up destroying the citric acid and the berries start to lose their fresh taste, it can be revived a bit with some additional lemon or lime juice or with some powdered citric acid.

MIXED BERRY

In a saucepan, combine the sugar and 1 cup (235 ml) of the water. Heat over medium-high heat until the sugar has dissolved and the syrup begins to boil. Remove the syrup from the heat and pour over the berries to macerate. Using a potato masher, crush the macerated berries to further release their juice. Using a fine-mesh strainer, strain out the fruit pulp and seeds from the syrup as fully as possible.

FOR THE SYRUP AND SELTZER METHOD Chill the syrup and add to carbonated water.

FOR STRAIGHT CARBONATION OR FERMENTATION Add the rest of the water to the strained syrup.

FOR STRAIGHT CARBONATION Chill the mixture before adding it to the keg or carbonator of your choice.

FOR FERMENTATION Hydrate the yeast in ¼ cup (60 ml) or less of warm water. Add the hydrated yeast to the mixture after it has cooled to 10 to 15°F (5.5 to 8°C) above room temperature. Stir in the yeast nutrient. Mix well and then bottle.

YIELD 1 GALLON (3.8 L)

Melon-flavored sodas can be a refreshing summer treat and pack a lot of fresh melon flavor. Keeping the heating to a minimum will preserve much of the fresh flavor, but it also makes any straight carbonation or syrup and seltzer recipes prone to natural fermentation if not stored properly. The addition of lemon is primarily for the citric acid in order to make the soda taste fruitier. Keep in mind, also, that the syrup will be thinner and therefore will dilute the carbonation from the seltzer more than usual. Regarding color: A lot of the bright red from watermelon comes from the pulp, so it's very noticeable when that starts to settle out, but a freshly mixed watermelon soda can be as appealing to the eyes as it is to the taste buds. For a more complex crushed melon flavor, use equal parts honeydew, cantaloupe, and watermelon, instead of watermelon alone, and cut the amount of lemon juice in half.

WATERMELON

In a saucepan, combine the sugar, half of the lemon juice, and 1 cup (235 ml) of the water. Heat over medium-high heat and let boil for about 5 minutes. Remove the syrup from the heat and pour over the diced melon to macerate. Using a potato masher, crush the macerated melon to further release its juice. Using a fine-mesh strainer, strain out the fruit pulp and seeds from the syrup as fully as possible.

FOR THE SYRUP AND SELTZER METHOD Add the rest of the lemon juice, chill the syrup, and add to carbonated water.

FOR STRAIGHT CARBONATION OR FERMENTATION Add the rest of the water and lemon juice to the strained syrup.

FOR STRAIGHT CARBONATION Chill the mixture before adding it to the keg or carbonator of your choice.

FOR FERMENTATION Hydrate the yeast in ¼ cup (60 ml) or less of warm water. Add the hydrated yeast to the mixture after it has cooled to 10 to 15°F (5.5 to 8°C) above room temperature. Stir in the yeast nutrient. Mix well and then bottle.

YIELD 1 GALLON (3.8 L)

SYRUP + SELTZER

2 cups (400 g) sugar

½ cup (120 ml) fresh lemon juice

1 cup (235 ml) water

4 pounds (1.8 kg) diced watermelon

(syrup for 1 gallon [3.8 L] finished soda; use 4 to 6 tablespoons [60 to 90 ml] per 8 ounces [235 ml] carbonated water, or to taste)

STRAIGHT CARBONATION

2 cups (400 g) sugar

½ cup (120 ml) fresh lemon juice

11½ cups (2.7 L) water

4 pounds (1.8 kg) diced watermelon

FERMENTATION

2¼ cups (450 g) sugar

½ cup (120 ml) fresh lemon juice

11½ cups (2.7 L) water

4 pounds (1.8 kg) diced watermelon

⅛ teaspoon Champagne yeast

1 g yeast nutrient

roots &
herbal
teas

Sassafras is known as the original main component in traditional root beer. It fell out of use in commercial root beers because of its safrole content, which has been linked to cancer. Somehow, this has not deterred many from using sassafras root for teas, and it can be found in some health food stores that stock bulk herbs. It is usually available in cut and sifted form or in powdered form. The powdered form can be difficult to work with when straining. This recipe is straight sassafras and is a sweetened and carbonated version of the traditional sassafras tea. When using the natural root alone for root beer, many will find that the flavor differs from the off-the-shelf versions that they are accustomed to drinking. It can have an earthy or bitter flavor. When steeping, I find that bringing the water to a boil, then adding the bark and allowing it to steep for a number of hours, will bring the best flavor and a deep red color to the sassafras brew.

SASSAFRAS

In a saucepan, combine the root and water. For the syrup and seltzer method, use 1 cup (235 ml) water; otherwise, use as much water as is practical to strain. Bring to a boil and then remove from the heat and let steep for 30 to 60 minutes. Strain out the root and return the water to the saucepan. Add the sugar and heat to dissolve and then remove the syrup from the heat.

FOR THE SYRUP AND SELTZER METHOD Chill the syrup and add to carbonated water.

FOR STRAIGHT CARBONATION OR FERMENTATION Add the rest of the water to the strained syrup.

FOR STRAIGHT CARBONATION Chill the mixture before adding it to the keg or carbonator of your choice.

FOR FERMENTATION Hydrate the yeast in ¼ cup (60 ml) or less of warm water. Add the hydrated yeast to the mixture after it has cooled to 10 to 15°F (5.5 to 8°C) above room temperature. Stir in the yeast nutrient. Mix well and then bottle.

YIELD 1 GALLON (3.8 L)

SYRUP + SELTZER

2 tablespoons (15 g) sassafras root bark powder or ¼ cup (28 g) cut and sifted bark

1 cup (235 ml) water

2 cups (400 g) sugar

(syrup for 1 gallon [3.8 L] finished soda; use 1½ to 2 tablespoons [25 to 28 ml] per 8 ounces [235 ml] carbonated water, or to taste)

STRAIGHT CARBONATION

2 tablespoons (15 g) sassafras root bark powder or ¼ cup (28 g) cut and sifted bark

15 cups (3.5 L) water

2 cups (400 g) sugar

FERMENTATION

2 tablespoons (15 g) sassafras root bark powder or ¼ cup (28 g) cut and sifted bark

15 cups (3.5 L) water

2 cups (400 g) sugar

⅛ teaspoon Champagne yeast

1 g yeast nutrient

SYRUP + SELTZER

2 cups (400 g) sugar

1 cup (235 ml) water

1 tablespoon (20 g) molasses

1 teaspoon flavor base
(page 77)

½ teaspoon citric acid

(syrup for 1 gallon [3.8 L]
finished soda; use 1½ to 2
tablespoons [25 to 28 ml] per
8 ounces [235 ml] carbonated
water, or to taste)

STRAIGHT CARBONATION

2 cups (400 g) sugar

15 cups (3.5 L) water

1 tablespoon (20 g) molasses

1 teaspoon flavor base
(page 77)

½ teaspoon citric acid

FERMENTATION

2 cups (400 g) sugar

15 cups (3.5 L) water

1 tablespoon (20 g) molasses

1 teaspoon flavor base
(page 77)

½ teaspoon citric acid

⅛ teaspoon Champagne yeast

1.5 g yeast nutrient

The original colas were created at the pharmacy in the days when druggists kept formulas on hand for everything from cough remedies to piano polish. So while this recipe may not exactly be the top-secret formula for the nerve tonic that has evolved into that red and white can known the world over, the method for making it at home is similar to what would have been done in the corner drug store all those years ago. When using essential oils, make sure they are intended for food use, not just for aromatherapy. When this cola is fermenting, the oils put a little bit more stress on the yeast so it takes a little bit longer and it's a good idea to use a little extra yeast nutrient. Phosphoric acid will bring the flavor closer to a commercial cola, but food-grade phosphoric acid can be hard to find and difficult to work with safely.

ESSENTIAL COLA

In a saucepan, combine the sugar, water, and molasses, heating until dissolved. For the syrup and seltzer method, use 1 cup (235 ml) water; otherwise, use it all. Allow the syrup or mixture to cool and then add the flavor base and citric acid.

FOR THE SYRUP AND SELTZER METHOD Chill the syrup and add to carbonated water.

FOR STRAIGHT CARBONATION Chill the mixture before adding it to the keg or carbonator of your choice.

FOR FERMENTATION Hydrate the yeast in ¼ cup (60 ml) or less of warm water. Add the hydrated yeast to the mixture after it has cooled to 10 to 15°F (5.5 to 8°C) above room temperature. Stir in the yeast nutrient. Mix well and then bottle.

YIELD 1 GALLON (3.8 L)

TECHNIQUE
FLAVOR BASES WITH ESSENTIAL OILS

Making a flavor base using essential oils is one alternative to using artificial extracts. The key is finding a carrier that the oils will dissolve into so that they will stay dissolved in the finished beverage. One option is to add the drops of oils to a small amount of alcohol. The other is to use an emulsifier such as gum arabic to make them water soluble.

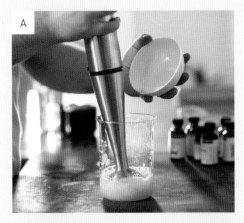

1. Using a handheld mixer, make a slurry of the gum arabic by slowly adding it to the water while mixing. **(A)**

2. After the gum is well dissolved and there are no fish eyes (undissolved clumps), add the oils to the slurry. An easy way to measure them correctly is with a graduated pipette. Disposable pipettes are available online and are inexpensive in small quantities. Blend again to disperse the flavoring oils. **(B)**

3. After blending, the base can be added to a syrup and the oils should remain emulsified with the water in the beverage. **(C)**

    Flavor base for 5 gallons (19 L):
    3 ml orange oil
    2.5 ml lime oil
    1.25 ml cinnamon oil
    1 ml lemon oil
    1 ml nutmeg oil
    1 ml orange blossom oil
    0.5 ml lavender oil
    1 ml pure anise extract
    ¼ teaspoon pure vanilla extract
    10 g gum arabic
    100 ml water

SYRUP + SELTZER

2 cups (475 ml) water

2 cups (400 g) sugar

¼ teaspoon citric acid

1 tablespoon (20 g) molasses

Herbal Blend (below)

(syrup for 1 gallon [3.8 L] finished soda; use 1½ to 2 tablespoons [25 to 28 ml] per 8 ounces [235 ml] carbonated water, or to taste)

STRAIGHT CARBONATION

15 cups (3.5 L) water

2 cups (400 g) sugar

¼ teaspoon citric acid

1 tablespoon (20 g) molasses

Herbal Blend (below)

FERMENTATION

15 cups (3.5 L) water

2¼ cups (450 g) sugar

¼ teaspoon citric acid

1 tablespoon (20 g) molasses

Herbal Blend (below)

⅛ teaspoon Champagne yeast

1 g yeast nutrient

HERBAL BLEND

Zest of 2 oranges

Zest of 1 lemon

Zest of 1 lime

2 sections star anise

1 teaspoon each dried lavender flowers and ground nutmeg

½ teaspoon ground cardamom

¼ teaspoon ground cinnamon

1 (2-inch, or 5 cm) piece fresh ginger, sliced

1 (6-inch, or 15 cm) vanilla bean, split

For those with little interest in measuring out minute amounts of specialty flavored oils, a good cola can be made with herbs and spices as well. This will have a little bit more of an earthy flavor than the essential oil version, but the outcome is otherwise pretty comparable. Similar to the essential oil recipe, this one omits the phosphoric acid, but the overall flavor is still characteristic of cola.

HERBAL COLA

In a saucepan, combine the water, zests, star anise, lavender, nutmeg, cardamom, cinnamon, ginger, and vanilla. For the syrup and seltzer method, use 2 cups (475 ml) water; otherwise, use as much water as is practical to strain. Bring to a boil and then remove from the heat and let steep for 20 to 30 minutes. Strain out the spices and return the water to the saucepan. Add the sugar, citric acid, and molasses and heat to dissolve. Then remove the syrup from the heat.

FOR THE SYRUP AND SELTZER METHOD Chill the syrup and add to carbonated water.

FOR STRAIGHT CARBONATION OR FERMENTATION Add the rest of the water to the strained syrup.

FOR STRAIGHT CARBONATION Chill the mixture before adding it to the keg or carbonator of your choice.

FOR FERMENTATION Hydrate the yeast in ¼ cup (60 ml) or less of warm water. Add the hydrated yeast to the mixture after it has cooled to 10 to 15°F (5.5 to 8°C) above room temperature. Stir in the yeast nutrient. Mix well and then bottle.

YIELD 1 GALLON (3.8 L)

RECIPE VARIANT

Crush in 4–5 maraschino cherries with the citrus zest or add in ½ teaspoon cherry or almond extract for a cherry cola.

SYRUP + SELTZER

2 cups (475 ml) water

½ cup (20 g) dried hibiscus flowers

½ teaspoon ground ginger

2 cups (400 g) granulated or (384 g) turbinado sugar

(syrup for 1 gallon [3.8 L] finished soda; use 2 to 4 tablespoons [28 to 60 ml] per 8 ounces [235 ml] carbonated water, or to taste)

STRAIGHT CARBONATION

15 cups (3.5 L) water

½ cup (20 g) dried hibiscus flowers

½ teaspoon ground ginger

2 cups (400 g) granulated or (384 g) turbinado sugar

FERMENTATION

15 cups (3.5 L) water

½ cup (20 g) dried hibiscus flowers

½ teaspoon ginger paste

2¼ cups (450 g) granulated or (432 g) turbinado sugar

⅛ teaspoon Champagne yeast

0.5 g yeast nutrient

Jamaica is a Mexican drink that is categorized as an agua fresca and falls in the same group as horchata. Its primary flavor and deep red color comes from hibiscus flowers, which have a floral but subtly fruity flavor. It is often mildly spiced to complement this flavor. This version includes some ginger but otherwise lets the hibiscus flavor dominate.

JAMAICA (HIBISCUS)

In a saucepan, combine the water, hibiscus flowers, and ginger. For the syrup and seltzer method, use 2 cups (475 ml) water; otherwise, use as much water as is practical to strain. Bring to a boil and then remove from the heat and let steep for 30 to 60 minutes. Strain out the spices and return the water to the saucepan. Add the sugar and heat until dissolved. Remove the syrup from the heat.

FOR THE SYRUP AND SELTZER METHOD Chill the syrup and add to carbonated water.

FOR STRAIGHT CARBONATION OR FERMENTATION Add the rest of the water to the strained syrup.

FOR STRAIGHT CARBONATION Chill the mixture before adding it to the keg or carbonator of your choice.

FOR FERMENTATION Hydrate the yeast in ¼ cup (60 ml) or less of warm water. Add the hydrated yeast to the mixture after it has cooled to 10 to 15°F (5.5 to 8°C) above room temperature. Stir in the yeast nutrient. Mix well and then bottle.

YIELD 1 GALLON (3.8 L)

SYRUP + SELTZER

½ tablespoon cut and sifted sarsaparilla root

½ tablespoon wintergreen leaves

1 cup (235 ml) water

2 cups (450 g) lightly packed light brown sugar

2 teaspoons pure vanilla extract

(syrup for 1 gallon [3.8 L] finished soda; use 1½ to 2 tablespoons [25 to 28 ml] per 8 ounces [235 ml] carbonated water, or to taste)

STRAIGHT CARBONATION

½ tablespoon cut and sifted sarsaparilla root

½ tablespoon wintergreen leaves

15 cups (3.5 L) water

2 cups (450 g) lightly packed light brown sugar

2 teaspoons pure vanilla extract

FERMENTATION

½ tablespoon cut and sifted sarsaparilla root

½ tablespoon wintergreen leaves

15 cups (3.5 L) water

2¼ cups (510 g) lightly packed light brown sugar

2 teaspoons pure vanilla extract

⅛ teaspoon Champagne yeast

0.5 g yeast nutrient

Sarsaparilla was sold as a tonic for various purposes near the turn of the twentieth century. Despite sarsaparilla being the namesake root for the tonic, it often included a number of herbals. Sarsaparilla root varieties can come from different species of the plant. The Mexican and Indian varieties are the most prevalent. In my experience, the Mexican variety has a slightly bitter taste, while the Indian variety is a bit sweeter and slightly more floral.

SARSAPARILLA

In a saucepan, combine the root, wintergreen, and water. For the syrup and seltzer method, use 1 cup (235 ml) water; otherwise, use as much water as is practical to strain. Bring to a boil and then remove from the heat and let steep for 30 to 60 minutes. Strain out the roots and return the water to the saucepan. Add the sugar and heat until dissolved. Then remove the syrup from the heat.

FOR THE SYRUP AND SELTZER METHOD Chill the syrup, add the vanilla, and add to carbonated water.

FOR STRAIGHT CARBONATION OR FERMENTATION Add the rest of the water plus the vanilla to the strained syrup.

FOR STRAIGHT CARBONATION Chill the mixture before adding it to the keg or carbonator of your choice.

FOR FERMENTATION Hydrate the yeast in ¼ cup (60 ml) or less of warm water. Add the hydrated yeast to the mixture after it has cooled to 10 to 15°F (5.5 to 8°C) above room temperature. Stir in the yeast nutrient. Mix well and then bottle.

YIELD 1 GALLON (3.8 L)

Rose water has long been used in culinary applications, particularly in Middle Eastern cuisine. It's more of an aroma than a flavor, so it comes out very subtly when added to soda. This recipe pairs it with apple and vanilla for a very light and refreshing soda that's not too sweet.

APPLE ROSE

In a saucepan, combine the sugar and water and heat until dissolved. For the syrup and seltzer method, use 1 cup (235 ml) water; otherwise, use it all. Remove from the heat and add the apple juice. Allow the syrup or mixture to cool and then add the rose water and vanilla.

FOR THE SYRUP AND SELTZER METHOD Chill the syrup and add to carbonated water.

FOR STRAIGHT CARBONATION Chill the mixture before adding it to the keg or carbonator of your choice.

FOR FERMENTATION Hydrate the yeast in ¼ cup (60 ml) or less of warm water. Add the hydrated yeast to the mixture after it has cooled to 10 to 15°F (5.5 to 8°C) above room temperature. Stir in the yeast nutrient. Mix well and then bottle.

YIELD 1 GALLON (3.8 L)

SYRUP + SELTZER

1¾ cups (336 g) turbinado sugar

1 cup (235 ml) water

½ cup (120 ml) apple juice concentrate

2 teaspoons rose water

¼ teaspoon pure vanilla extract

(syrup for 1 gallon [3.8 L] finished soda; use 2 to 3 tablespoons [28 to 45 ml] per 8 ounces [235 ml] carbonated water, or to taste)

STRAIGHT CARBONATION

1¾ cups (336 g) turbinado sugar

14½ cups (3.4 L) water

½ cup (120 ml) apple juice concentrate

2 teaspoons rose water

¼ teaspoon pure vanilla extract

FERMENTATION

2 cups (384 g) turbinado sugar

14½ cups (3.4 L) water

¾ cup (175 ml) apple juice concentrate

3 teaspoons (15 ml) rose water

¼ teaspoon pure vanilla extract

⅛ teaspoon Champagne yeast

1 g yeast nutrient

RECIPE VARIANT

Many edible flowers pair well with mellow fruits. Pear and lavender make a good combination, as do white grape and elderflower. These flowers can be steeped directly instead of using rose water. For a little brighter flavor, I like orange and marigold.

One great thing about root beer is its customizability. It can be simple like the sassafras and sarsaparilla recipes on pages 75 and 82, or it can be as complicated as desired. This recipe has many of the roots common to different varieties of root beer. When making a recipe like this with ingredients that may be unfamiliar, it's usually a good idea to steep a little of each ingredient separately for a taste test. That way, if any of the individual flavors are glaringly undesirable, they can be omitted. The yucca root, for instance, is included for a frothier head, but it does impart a slightly bitter flavor.

MULTI-ROOT BEER

In a saucepan, combine the water, roots, spices, and herbs. For the syrup and seltzer method, use 2 cups (475 ml) water; otherwise, use as much water as is practical to strain. Bring to a boil and then remove from the heat and let steep for 30 to 60 minutes. Strain out the spices and return the water to the saucepan. Add the sugar and heat until dissolved. Remove the syrup from the heat.

FOR THE SYRUP AND SELTZER METHOD Chill the syrup and add to carbonated water.

FOR STRAIGHT CARBONATION OR FERMENTATION Add the rest of the water to the strained syrup.

FOR STRAIGHT CARBONATION Chill the mixture before adding it to the keg or carbonator of your choice.

FOR FERMENTATION Hydrate the yeast in ¼ cup (60 ml) or less of warm water. Add the hydrated yeast to the mixture after it has cooled to 10 to 15°F (5.5 to 8°C) above room temperature. Stir in the yeast nutrient. Mix well and then bottle.

YIELD 1 GALLON (3.8 L)

SYRUP + SELTZER

2 cups (475 ml) water

2 cups (450 g) lightly packed light brown sugar

Root Blend (below)

(syrup for 1 gallon [3.8 L] finished soda; use 2 to 4 tablespoons [28 to 60 ml] per 8 ounces [235 ml] carbonated water, or to taste)

STRAIGHT CARBONATION

15 cups (3.5 L) water

2 cups (450 g) lightly packed light brown sugar

Root Blend (below)

FERMENTATION

15 cups (3.5 L) water

2¼ cups (510 g) lightly packed light brown sugar

Root Blend (below)

⅛ teaspoon Champagne yeast

0.5 g yeast nutrient

ROOT BLEND

1 tablespoon (7 g) cut and sifted sassafras root bark

1 tablespoon (7 g) cut and sifted licorice root

½ tablespoon cut and sifted dandelion root

1 teaspoon cut and sifted yucca root

½ teaspoon cut and sifted sarsaparilla root

½ teaspoon cut and sifted wild cherry bark

1 section star anise

½ tablespoon wintergreen leaves

1 (1½-inch, or 3.7 cm) piece vanilla bean, split

1 teaspoon ginger paste

SYRUP + SELTZER

1 cup (235 ml) water

1 cup (200 g) granulated sugar

1 cup (225 g) lightly packed light brown sugar

5 teaspoons (25 ml) root beer concentrate

(syrup for 1 gallon [3.8 L] finished soda; use 1½ to 2 tablespoons [25 to 28 ml] per 8 ounces [235 ml] carbonated water, or to taste)

STRAIGHT CARBONATION

15 cups (3.5 L) water

1 cup (200 g) granulated sugar

1 cup (225 g) lightly packed light brown sugar

5 teaspoons (25 ml) root beer concentrate

FERMENTATION

15 cups (3.5 L) water

1¼ cups (250 g) granulated sugar

1 cup (225 g) lightly packed light brown sugar

5 teaspoons (25 ml) root beer concentrate

⅛ teaspoon Champagne yeast

1 g yeast nutrient

Though root beer can be a really fun thing to make completely from scratch, it can also be very tedious, and with so many ingredients it can be a challenge to get right. Extracts might not offer much flexibility, but they can make things much easier. However, even an extract recipe can be jazzed up and customized to personal preference. Adding vanilla, molasses, various sugars, wintergreen, or anise can bring a bland extract or concentrate back into line with expectations or individual taste. Commonly available root beer extracts and concentrates are available at the grocery or home-brew store from brands like McCormick, Watkins, Zatarain's, Gnome, and Rainbow. I usually like to use 1 ounce (28 ml) per 1 gallon (3.8 L), but this may vary depending on the brand.

EXTRACT ROOT BEER

In a saucepan, combine the water and sugars and heat until dissolved. For the syrup and seltzer method, use 1 cup (235 ml) water; otherwise, use it all. Remove from the heat and allow the syrup or mixture to cool. Add the root beer concentrate.

FOR THE SYRUP AND SELTZER METHOD Chill the syrup and add to carbonated water.

FOR STRAIGHT CARBONATION Chill the mixture before adding it to the keg or carbonator of your choice.

FOR FERMENTATION Hydrate the yeast in ¼ cup (60 ml) or less of warm water. Add the hydrated yeast to the mixture after it has cooled to 10 to 15°F (5.5 to 8°C) above room temperature. Stir in the yeast nutrient. Mix well and then bottle.

YIELD 1 GALLON (3.8 L)

Black licorice is very much a polarizing flavor. Some love it, some despise it, but there's not much middle ground. The traditional flavor comes not only from the root, but also from anise and a portion from molasses. All three are common ingredients in traditional root beers. This recipe features them prominently and almost exclusively for a classic treat. I like to add some burdock root for a slightly more complex flavor.

BLACK LICORICE

In a saucepan, bring 1 cup (235 ml) of the water to a boil and then remove from the heat. Add the roots to the saucepan and let steep for at least 1 hour. Strain to remove the roots as completely as possible. Add the sugar and molasses to the strained liquid and heat over medium-high heat until the sugar has dissolved. Remove from the heat and chill. Once cooled to room temperature or lower, add the anise extract.

FOR THE SYRUP AND SELTZER METHOD Chill the syrup and add to carbonated water.

FOR STRAIGHT CARBONATION OR FERMENTATION Add the rest of the water to the syrup.

FOR STRAIGHT CARBONATION Chill the mixture before adding it to the keg or carbonator of your choice.

FOR FERMENTATION Hydrate the yeast in ¼ cup (60 ml) or less of warm water. Add the hydrated yeast to the mixture after it has cooled to 10 to 15°F (5.5 to 8°C) above room temperature. Stir in the yeast nutrient. Mix well and then bottle.

YIELD 1 GALLON (3.8 L)

SYRUP + SELTZER

1 cup (235 ml) water

1 tablespoon (7 g) cut and sifted licorice root

½ tablespoon cut and sifted burdock root

2 cups (400 g) sugar

¼ cup (80 g) molasses

½ teaspoon pure anise extract

(syrup for 1 gallon [3.8 L] finished soda; use 1½ to 2 tablespoons [25 to 28 ml] per 8 ounces [235 ml] carbonated water, or to taste)

STRAIGHT CARBONATION

15 cups (3.5 L) water

1 tablespoon (7 g) cut and sifted licorice root

½ tablespoon cut and sifted burdock root

2 cups (400 g) sugar

¼ cup (80 g) molasses

½ teaspoon pure anise extract

FERMENTATION

15 cups (3.5 L) water

1 tablespoon (7 g) cut and sifted licorice root

½ tablespoon cut and sifted burdock root

2¼ cups (450 g) sugar

¼ cup (80 g) molasses

½ teaspoon pure anise extract

⅛ teaspoon Champagne yeast

1 g yeast nutrient

½ tablespoon ginger paste

5 fluid ounces (150 ml) fresh lemon juice or the juice and zest of 2 lemons

1 cup (235 ml) water

2 cups (400 g) sugar (syrup for 1 gallon [3.8 L] finished soda; use 2 to 3 tablespoons [28 to 45 ml] per 8 ounces [235 ml] carbonated water, or to taste)

STRAIGHT CARBONATION

Thumb-size piece fresh ginger or ½ tablespoon ginger paste

5 fluid ounces (150 ml) fresh lemon juice or the juice and zest of 2 lemons

14½ cups (3.4 L) water

2 cups (400 g) sugar

FERMENTATION

Thumb-size piece fresh ginger, sliced or grated

5 fluid ounces (150 ml) fresh lemon juice or the juice and zest of 2 lemons

14 cups (3.3 L) water

2¼ cups (450 g) sugar

⅛ teaspoon Champagne yeast

0.5 g yeast nutrient

Ginger ale is named as such because it shares its roots (no pun intended) with beer making. A ginger ale is typically more citrusy and not as spicy as a ginger beer, though this recipe can easily be adjusted according to taste by varying the amount of ginger. Fresh ginger or ginger paste (found in the produce aisle, near the herbs) works equally well, though ginger pastes can sometimes have preservatives that make fermentation difficult or impossible. For a spicier ginger kick, leave a small chunk of diced ginger in the bottom of the bottle.

GINGER ALE

In a saucepan, combine the ginger, zest (if using), and water. For the syrup and seltzer method, use 1 cup (235 ml) water; otherwise, use as much water as is practical to strain. Bring to a boil and then remove from the heat and let steep for 10 to 15 minutes. Strain out the ginger and return the water to the saucepan. Add the sugar and 1 tablespoon (15 ml) of the lemon juice and bring to a boil over medium-high heat. Let boil for about 5 minutes. Remove the syrup from the heat and add the rest of the juice.

FOR THE SYRUP AND SELTZER METHOD Chill the syrup and add to carbonated water.

FOR STRAIGHT CARBONATION OR FERMENTATION Add the rest of the water to the syrup.

FOR STRAIGHT CARBONATION Chill the mixture before adding it to the keg or carbonator of your choice.

FOR FERMENTATION Hydrate the yeast in ¼ cup (60 ml) or less of warm water. Add the hydrated yeast to the mixture after it has cooled to 10 to 15°F (5.5 to 8°C) above room temperature. Stir in the yeast nutrient. Mix well and then bottle.

YIELD 1 GALLON (3.8 L)

SYRUP + SELTZER

4 teaspoons (10 g) cut and sifted dandelion root

2 teaspoons cut and sifted burdock root

½ teaspoon ginger paste

1 cup (235 ml) water

2 cups (400 g) sugar

2 teaspoons molasses

(syrup for 1 gallon [3.8 L] finished soda; use 1½ to 2 tablespoons [25 to 28 ml] per 8 ounces [235 ml] carbonated water, or to taste)

STRAIGHT CARBONATION

4 teaspoons (10 g) cut and sifted dandelion root

2 teaspoons cut and sifted burdock root

½ teaspoon ginger paste

14 cups (3.3 L) water

2 cups (400 g) sugar

2 teaspoons molasses

FERMENTATION

4 teaspoons (10 g) cut and sifted dandelion root

2 teaspoons cut and sifted burdock root

½ teaspoon ginger paste

14 cups (3.3 L) water

2¼ cups (450 g) sugar

2 teaspoons molasses

⅛ teaspoon Champagne yeast

0.5 g yeast nutrient

Dandelion & burdock is a drink that is popular in the United Kingdom. It has some similarities to the American root beer, but it has a distinctly different taste. Burdock root offers a bitter, somewhat earthy flavor, while dandelion serves up a sweeter base that blends well with the ginger and molasses. The resulting beverage is a seemingly more sophisticated, old-world take on the traditional root beer.

DANDELION & BURDOCK

In a saucepan, combine the roots, ginger, and water. For the syrup and seltzer method, use 1 cup (235 ml) water; otherwise, use as much water as is practical to strain. Bring to a boil and then remove from the heat and let steep for 30 to 60 minutes. Strain out the root and return the water to the saucepan. Add the sugar and molasses and heat until dissolved. Then remove the syrup from the heat.

FOR THE SYRUP AND SELTZER METHOD Chill the syrup and add to carbonated water.

FOR STRAIGHT CARBONATION OR FERMENTATION Add the rest of the water to the strained syrup.

FOR STRAIGHT CARBONATION Chill the mixture before adding it to the keg or carbonator of your choice.

FOR FERMENTATION Hydrate the yeast in ¼ cup (60 ml) or less of warm water. Add the hydrated yeast to the mixture after it has cooled to 10 to 15°F (5.5 to 8°C) above room temperature. Stir in the yeast nutrient. Mix well and then bottle.

YIELD 1 GALLON (3.8 L)

My sister drew her inspiration for this drink from a trip to Paris, where she was served water that was lightly flavored with mint leaves and lemon. This version is not as subtle on the flavors but still holds a sophisticated old-world charm. Mint flavoring can be added in the form of herbal tea bags, fresh mint leaves, or mint extract. Each one gives a slight difference in flavor and color, but they all work equally well.

LEMON MINT

In a saucepan, combine the sugar, ½ cup (120 ml) of the water, and 2 tablespoons (28 ml) of the lemon juice. Heat over medium-high heat until the sugar has dissolved and the syrup has boiled for about 5 minutes. If using tea bags or mint leaves, steep in 2 cups (475 ml) hot water, separately. Remove the syrup from the heat and add the mint tea and remaining lemon juice as the syrup cools. If using mint extract, add it to syrup after it has cooled to room temperature or cooler.

FOR THE SYRUP AND SELTZER METHOD Chill the syrup and add to carbonated water.

FOR STRAIGHT CARBONATION OR FERMENTATION Add the rest of the water to the syrup.

FOR STRAIGHT CARBONATION Chill the mixture before adding it to the keg or carbonator of your choice.

FOR FERMENTATION Hydrate the yeast in ¼ cup (60 ml) or less of warm water. Add the hydrated yeast to the mixture after it has cooled to 10 to 15°F (5.5 to 8°C) above room temperature. Stir in the yeast nutrient. Mix well and then bottle.

YIELD 1 GALLON (3.8 L)

SYRUP + SELTZER

2 cups (400 g) sugar

½ cup (120 ml) water

½ cup (120 ml) fresh lemon juice or the juice and zest of 2 lemons

½ teaspoon pure mint extract, 2 mint herbal tea bags, or 15 to 20 fresh mint leaves

(syrup for 1 gallon [3.8 L] finished soda; use 2 to 3 tablespoons [28 to 45 ml] per 8 ounces [235 ml] carbonated water, or to taste)

STRAIGHT CARBONATION

2 cups (400 g) sugar

14½ cups (3.4 L) water

½ cup (120 ml) fresh lemon juice or the juice and zest of 2 lemons

½ teaspoon pure mint extract, 2 mint herbal tea bags, or 15 to 20 fresh mint leaves

FERMENTATION

2¼ cups (450 g) sugar

14½ cups (3.4 L) water

½ cup (120 ml) fresh lemon juice or the juice and zest of 2 lemons

½ teaspoon pure mint extract, 3 mint herbal tea bags, or 20 to 25 fresh mint leaves

⅛ teaspoon Champagne yeast

1 g yeast nutrient

SYRUP + SELTZER

2 cups (475 ml) water

2 cups (400 g) sugar

½ teaspoon citric acid

½ tablespoon molasses

1 tablespoon (15 ml) pure almond extract

Fruit and Spice Blend (opposite)

(syrup for 1 gallon [3.8 L] finished soda; use 2 to 4 tablespoons [28 to 60 ml] per 8 ounces [235 ml] carbonated water, or to taste)

STRAIGHT CARBONATION

15 cups (3.5 L) water

2 cups (400 g) sugar

½ teaspoon citric acid

½ tablespoon molasses

1 tablespoon (15 ml) pure almond extract

Fruit and Spice Blend (opposite)

FERMENTATION

15 cups (3.5 L) water

2¼ cups (450 g) sugar

½ teaspoon citric acid

½ tablespoon molasses

1 tablespoon (15 ml) pure almond extract

Fruit and Spice Blend (opposite)

⅛ teaspoon Champagne yeast

0.5 g yeast nutrient

The Dr. has kept his unique formula of 23 flavors secret for nearly 130 years, and while there are a number of knockoffs under private-label brands, there are few recipes for a homemade version that do it justice. An antique druggist's formula book was brought to light a few years ago with what may be an early version of the original formula. The bitters formula included gentian root and cardamom, but otherwise that's really all that made it into my recipe. I know that the company has denied rumors that the drink contains prune juice, but that doesn't mean it doesn't have somewhat of a plum flavor. In fact, a lot of drupe fruits' flavors have been nominated for a position among the mysterious 23, but regardless, they all share similarities that I think are pretty much covered here by the dried plums (yes, prunes) and the almond extract.

MOCKTER PEPPER

In a saucepan, combine the water, fruit, spices, herbs, and roots. For the syrup and seltzer method, use 2 cups (475 ml) water; otherwise, use as much water as is practical to strain. Bring to a boil and then remove from the heat and let steep for 30 to 60 minutes. Strain out the solid ingredients and return the water to the saucepan. Add the sugar, citric acid, and molasses and heat until dissolved. Remove the syrup from the heat.

FOR THE SYRUP AND SELTZER METHOD Chill the syrup, add the almond extract, and add to carbonated water.

FOR STRAIGHT CARBONATION OR FERMENTATION Add the rest of the water plus the almond extract to the strained syrup.

FOR STRAIGHT CARBONATION Chill the mixture before adding it to the keg or carbonator of your choice.

FOR FERMENTATION Hydrate the yeast in ¼ cup (60 ml) or less of warm water. Add the hydrated yeast to the mixture after it has cooled to 10 to 15°F (5.5 to 8°C) above room temperature. Stir in the yeast nutrient. Mix well and then bottle.

YIELD 1 GALLON (3.8 L)

FRUIT AND SPICE BLEND

½ cup (88 g) dried plums (prunes)

½ cup (65 g) raspberries

1 (3-inch, or 7.5 cm) piece vanilla bean, split

1 tablespoon (6 g) wintergreen leaves

½ tablespoon whole cloves

6 sections star anise

1 teaspoon ginger paste

1 teaspoon ground nutmeg

½ teaspoon ground cardamom

½ teaspoon ground cinnamon

½ teaspoon cut and sifted wild cherry bark

¼ teaspoon cut and sifted gentian root

indulgent

I've heard or read about a few variations on cream soda's origins, and I'm not entirely sure which is accurate. Regardless, vanilla gives the creamy notes and is the main flavoring component in this cream soda. Pure vanilla extract and caramelized sugar give an artisan charm to this cream soda that is sure to please any palate. Real vanilla beans are an option, but they can be difficult to work with when infusing the flavor into just water. Imitation vanilla can be used, but it really leaves something to be desired. Adding grenadine, some syrup from a jar of maraschino cherries, or simply some almond flavoring and food coloring will give an approximation of the red cream soda that is popular in Canada and elsewhere.

VANILLA CREAM

In a saucepan, bring the water with the vanilla bean (if using) to a boil. For the syrup and seltzer method, use 1 cup (235 ml) water; otherwise, use as much water as is practical to strain. Let boil for about 5 minutes and then remove from the heat and let steep for 20 minutes. Let cool and then strain out the vanilla bean and set the infused water aside. In a second saucepan, heat the sugar over medium heat while stirring constantly. When the sugar has turned a honey/amber color, add 1 cup (235 ml) water. The water will immediately boil as the sugar cools and dissolves. Continue to heat over low or medium heat until the sugar is completely dissolved. Let cool.

FOR THE SYRUP AND SELTZER METHOD Chill the syrup, add the vanilla-infused water or the extract, and add to carbonated water.

FOR STRAIGHT CARBONATION OR FERMENTATION Add the rest of the water and the vanilla-infused water or the extract to the syrup.

FOR STRAIGHT CARBONATION Chill the mixture before adding it to the keg or carbonator of your choice.

FOR FERMENTATION Hydrate the yeast in ¼ cup (60 ml) or less of warm water. Add the hydrated yeast to the mixture after it has cooled to 10 to 15°F (5.5 to 8°C) above room temperature. Stir in the yeast nutrient. Mix well and then bottle.

YIELD 1 GALLON (3.8 L)

SYRUP + SELTZER

1 cup (235 ml) water

1½ teaspoons pure vanilla extract or 1 vanilla bean, split

2 cups (400 g) sugar

(syrup for 1 gallon [3.8 L] finished soda; use 1½ to 2 tablespoons [25 to 28 ml] per 8 ounces [235 ml] carbonated water, or to taste)

STRAIGHT CARBONATION

15 cups (3.5 L) water

1½ teaspoons pure vanilla extract or 1 vanilla bean, split

2 cups (400 g) sugar

FERMENTATION

15 cups (3.5 L) water

2 teaspoons pure vanilla extract or 1½ vanilla beans, split

2¼ cups (450 g) sugar

⅛ teaspoon Champagne yeast

1 g yeast nutrient

SYRUP + SELTZER

¼ cup (35 g) chocolate malt

2 cups (475 ml) water

2 cups (400 g) sugar

1 tablespoon (15 ml) chocolate extract

1½ teaspoons pure vanilla extract

(syrup for 1 gallon [3.8 L] finished soda; use 2 to 4 tablespoons [28 to 60 ml] per 8 ounces [235 ml] carbonated water, or to taste)

STRAIGHT CARBONATION

¼ cup (35 g) chocolate malt

15 cups (3.5 L) water

2 cups (400 g) sugar

1 tablespoon (15 ml) chocolate extract

1½ teaspoons pure vanilla extract

FERMENTATION

5 tablespoons (44 g) chocolate malt

15 cups (3.5 L) water

2¼ cups (450 g) sugar

1½ tablespoons (25 ml) chocolate extract

1½ teaspoons pure vanilla extract

⅛ teaspoon Champagne yeast

0.5 g yeast nutrient

Chocolate sodas are certainly a relic of the past. At the old-time soda fountain, though, a chocolate soda was quite common. These persisted in the early days of bottling but more or less died out at some point, possibly because the cocoa that would have been used in the chocolate syrup at the fountain was fine for a quick mix-and-drink, but it would have settled out in the bottle. That would have led soda bottlers to use artificial flavors that would have left them tasting like liquid Tootsie Rolls. I've long been on the lookout for something that tastes a little more like biting into a piece of chocolate than something artificial. In my search, I've found that the addition of a dark toasted malt (available from a home-brewing supply store) mimics the astringency of real chocolate. When the chocolate malt is used heavily, it can impart more of a mocha flavor. Adjust the grain component up or down as desired to suit your taste.

DARK CHOCOLATE

Using a grain mill, crack the chocolate malt. In a saucepan, bring the water to a boil and then remove from the heat. For the syrup and seltzer method, use 1 cup (235 ml) water; otherwise, use as much water as is practical to strain. Add the crushed grain and let steep for 20 minutes. Strain out the grain and return the water to the saucepan. Add the sugar and heat over medium-high heat until the sugar has dissolved.

FOR THE SYRUP AND SELTZER METHOD Chill the syrup, add the extracts, and add to carbonated water.

FOR STRAIGHT CARBONATION OR FERMENTATION Add the rest of the water and the extracts to the syrup.

FOR STRAIGHT CARBONATION Chill the mixture before adding it to the keg or carbonator of your choice.

FOR FERMENTATION Hydrate the yeast in ¼ cup (60 ml) or less of warm water. Add the hydrated yeast to the mixture after it has cooled to 10 to 15°F (5.5 to 8°C) above room temperature. Stir in the yeast nutrient. Mix well and then bottle.

YIELD 1 GALLON (3.8 L)

TECHNIQUE
STEEPING GRAINS

There are many different types of malts that are used as primary ingredients for brewing beer. Crystal or caramel malts are useful in soda making because they impart caramel, sweet, roasted, or chocolate flavor notes. If they are steeped incorrectly, they can cause bitter flavor notes from the tannins they contain.

1. Milling the grains allows the water to leach out more of the flavor components and gives better results for steeping. Any grain mill or coffee grinder will work, but grind the grain coarsely; it's difficult to strain if it's milled too finely or turned it into flour.

2. The water should be around 170°F (77°C) to avoid tannin extraction. The best way to measure is with a thermometer, but if one is not readily available, this is usually the temperature at which bubbles start to form and cling to the base of the pan. If they start to rise and the water begins to boil, it's too hot. Remove it from the heat just before it boils and add the grains.

3. Allow the grains to steep for 15 to 30 minutes. The color change in the water will become apparent immediately, but it will continue to darken as it sits. Strain out the grains before adding the flavored water to your syrup or sugar.

SYRUP + SELTZER

2 cups (400 g) sugar

1 cup (235 ml) water

¼ cup (60 ml) apple juice concentrate

(syrup for 1 gallon [3.8 L] finished soda; use 2 to 4 tablespoons [28 to 60 ml] per 8 ounces [235 ml] carbonated water, or to taste)

STRAIGHT CARBONATION

13½ cups (3.2 L) water

2 cups (400 g) sugar

1 cup (235 ml) 100% apple juice

FERMENTATION

13 cups (3.1 L) water

2¼ cups (450 g) sugar

1 cup (235 ml) 100% apple juice

⅛ teaspoon Champagne yeast

0.5 g yeast nutrient

FLAVOR AND JUICE BLEND

2 tablespoons (28 ml) fresh lemon juice

¾ cup (175 ml) strawberry-banana nectar

2 teaspoons pure vanilla extract

¼ teaspoon raspberry extract or ¼ cup (65 g) red raspberries

¼ teaspoon banana extract

¼ teaspoon pure almond extract

1 drop pure mint extract or 1 mint leaf

Who can recall childhood without a fond remembrance of chewy pink bubble gum? While this is a fruit flavor–based recipe, the added vanilla and touch of mint make this the "fantasy" candy flavor that is well known and loved. The main flavor components that give bubble gum its characteristic taste are raspberry, banana, and vanilla. The other fruits are included here to round out the tutti-frutti flavor (which literally means "all fruits"). This version is much fruitier than most pink pieces of gum, but it gives an added dimension to an age-old classic without being overbearing.

BUBBLE GUM

FOR THE SYRUP AND SELTZER METHOD Combine the sugar, water, and 1 tablespoon (15 ml) of the lemon juice in a saucepan. Bring to a boil and then remove from the heat. Add the remaining juices and juice concentrate and let cool to about room temperature. Add the extracts and mix well. Chill the syrup and add to carbonated water.

FOR THE STRAIGHT CARBONATION AND FERMENTATION METHODS Combine the berries, mint, and water in a saucepan using as much water as is practical to strain. Bring to a boil and then remove from the heat and let steep for 20 minutes. Mash the berries to remove their juices and then strain the pulp and return the water to the saucepan. Add the sugar and bring to a boil over medium-high heat. Remove from the heat and add the rest of the water along with the juice and extracts.

FOR STRAIGHT CARBONATION Chill the mixture before adding it to the keg or carbonator of your choice.

FOR FERMENTATION Hydrate the yeast in about ¼ cup (60 ml) or less of warm water. Add the yeast to the mixture after it has cooled to 10 to 15°F (5.5 to 8°C) above room temperature. Stir in the yeast nutrient. Mix well and then bottle.

YIELD 1 GALLON (3.8 L)

Horchata is a rice drink from Latin America that shares its lineage and characteristics with the Italian orzata. The Mexican version is flavored with cinnamon and vanilla. Like other aguas frescas, *it is usually served still over ice and sometimes contains actual milk. Fabulous horchata can be had in mom-and-pop taquerías and is best when it is homemade rather than from a mix. This recipe moves a little past the traditional and adds what I've always thought horchata was lacking: carbonation.*

HORCHATA

Soak the rice with the cinnamon in 4 cups (950 ml) of the water for at least 3 hours, or preferably overnight. After soaking, pulse in a blender a few times to break up the grains. Strain using a fine-mesh strainer 2 or 3 times until all the solids are removed.

In a saucepan, add the sugar to the strained rice water and bring to a boil; simmer for about 5 minutes. Allow the syrup to cool and then add the vanilla.

FOR THE SYRUP AND SELTZER METHOD Chill the syrup and add to carbonated water.

FOR STRAIGHT CARBONATION OR FERMENTATION Add the rest of the water to the syrup.

FOR STRAIGHT CARBONATION Chill the mixture before adding it to the keg or carbonator of your choice.

FOR FERMENTATION Hydrate the yeast in ¼ cup (60 ml) or less of warm water. Add the hydrated yeast to the mixture after it has cooled to 10 to 15°F (5.5 to 8°C) above room temperature. Stir in the yeast nutrient. Mix well and then bottle.

YIELD 1 GALLON (3.8 L)

SYRUP + SELTZER
½ cup (95 g) uncooked rice

¼ teaspoon ground cinnamon

4 cups (950 ml) water

2 cups (400 g) sugar

2 teaspoons pure vanilla extract

(syrup for 1 gallon [3.8 L] finished soda; use 3 to 5 tablespoons [45 to 75 ml] per 8 ounces [235 ml] carbonated water, or to taste)

STRAIGHT CARBONATION
½ cup (95 g) uncooked rice

¼ teaspoon ground cinnamon

15 cups (3.5 L) water

2 cups (400 g) sugar

2 teaspoons pure vanilla extract

FERMENTATION
½ cup (95 g) uncooked rice

¼ teaspoon cinnamon

15 cups (3.5 L) water

2 cups (400 g) sugar

2 teaspoons pure vanilla extract

⅛ teaspoon Champagne yeast

0.5 g yeast nutrient

A cousin to horchata, orzata, or orgeat, is made with almonds instead of rice. Orgeat syrup is known for lending flavor to its fair share of cocktails, such as the Mai Tai. It traditionally includes orange blossom water, but this version uses orange zest or orange juice, which will work just fine if orange blossom water isn't exactly a staple in the closest available pantry. If a floral note is a must, a touch of pure vanilla extract or rose water is an adequate substitute. Depending on the almonds and their freshness, the flavor they add may be variable. The addition of a small amount of almond extract boosts the flavor to where it needs to be.

ORZATA

Using a grain mill, coarsely grind the almonds. In a saucepan, bring the water to a boil. For the syrup and seltzer method, use 1 cup (235 ml) water; otherwise, use as much water as is practical to strain. Add the almonds and boil the mixture for 2 to 3 minutes. Remove from the heat and add the orange zest, if using. Let cool and then strain out the almonds and zest and return the water to the saucepan. Add the sugar and heat over medium-high heat until the sugar has dissolved.

FOR THE SYRUP AND SELTZER METHOD Chill the syrup, add the extract and juice concentrate, if using, and add to carbonated water.

FOR STRAIGHT CARBONATION OR FERMENTATION Add the rest of the water, the extracts, and the juice concentrate, if using, to the syrup.

FOR STRAIGHT CARBONATION Chill the mixture before adding it to the keg or carbonator of your choice.

FOR FERMENTATION Hydrate the yeast in ¼ cup (60 ml) or less of warm water. Add the hydrated yeast to the mixture after it has cooled to 10 to 15°F (5.5 to 8°C) above room temperature. Stir in the yeast nutrient. Mix well and then bottle.

YIELD 1 GALLON (3.8 L)

SYRUP + SELTZER

2 ounces (55 g) blanched almonds

1 cup (235 ml) water

Zest of ½ orange or ½ teaspoon orange juice concentrate

2 cups (400 g) sugar

¼ teaspoon pure almond extract

(syrup for 1 gallon [3.8 L] finished soda; use 2 to 3 tablespoons [28 to 45 ml] per 8 ounces [235 ml] carbonated water, or to taste)

STRAIGHT CARBONATION

2 ounces (55 g) blanched almonds

15 cups (3.5 L) water

Zest of ½ orange or ½ teaspoon orange juice concentrate

2 cups (400 g) sugar

¼ teaspoon pure almond extract

FERMENTATION

2 ounces (55 g) blanched almonds

15 cups (3.5 L) water

Zest of ½ orange or ½ teaspoon orange juice concentrate

2¼ cups (450 g) sugar

¼ teaspoon pure almond extract

⅛ teaspoon Champagne yeast

1 g yeast nutrient

Before a certain boy wizard made butterbeer enchanting to the Muggle crowd, there was actually historical reference to buttered beer. Recipes for such date as far back as the sixteenth and seventeenth centuries. This version is more akin to the butterscotch and butter rum flavors that are common in puddings and candies. The distinguishing characteristic from those flavors is that this contains a significant grain component, which in my opinion is what earns it the "beer" moniker. I prefer a lighter crystal malt for this, such as a 20L. If a darker malt is used, it's better to use less of it.

BUTTERBEER

Using a grain mill, crack the caramel malt. In a saucepan, bring the water to a boil and then remove from the heat. For the syrup and seltzer method, use 1 cup (235 ml) water; otherwise, use as much water as is practical to strain. Add the crushed grain and cinnamon and let steep for 20 minutes. Strain out the grain and return the water to the saucepan. (A coffee filter may be required for a final straining to remove any remaining cinnamon.) Add the sugar (or sugars) and heat over medium-high heat until the sugar has dissolved.

FOR THE SYRUP AND SELTZER METHOD Chill the syrup, add the extracts, and add to carbonated water.

FOR STRAIGHT CARBONATION OR FERMENTATION Add the rest of the water and the extracts to the syrup.

FOR STRAIGHT CARBONATION Chill the mixture before adding it to the keg or carbonator of your choice.

FOR FERMENTATION Hydrate the yeast in ¼ cup (60 ml) or less of warm water. Add the hydrated yeast to the mixture after it has cooled to 10 to 15°F (5.5 to 8°C) above room temperature. Stir in the yeast nutrient. Mix well and then bottle.

YIELD 1 GALLON (3.8 L)

holiday
recipes
for special
occasions

Cupcakes have been a big craze in the past few years, which has brought about not only a plethora of the handheld treats themselves but also everything from cupcake-flavored vodka to cupcake-flavored toothpaste. Why not have a cupcake soda? Caramel malt gives the baked flavor notes, while vanilla and almond simulate the frosting portion.

CUPCAKE

Using a grain mill, crack the caramel malt. In a saucepan, bring the water to a boil and then remove from the heat. For the syrup and seltzer method, use 1 cup (235 ml) water; otherwise, use as much water as is practical to strain. Add the crushed grain and let steep for 20 minutes. Strain out the grain and return the water to the saucepan. Add the sugar and heat over medium-high heat until the sugar has dissolved.

FOR THE SYRUP AND SELTZER METHOD Add the extracts, chill the syrup, and add to carbonated water.

FOR FERMENTATION AND STRAIGHT CARBONATION Add the extracts and the rest of the water to the syrup.

FOR STRAIGHT CARBONATION Chill the mixture before adding it to the keg or carbonator of your choice.

FOR FERMENTATION Hydrate the yeast in about ¼ cup (60 ml) or less of warm water. Add the yeast to the mixture after it has cooled to 10 to 15°F (5.5 to 8°C) above room temperature. Stir in the yeast nutrient. Mix well and then bottle.

YIELD 1 GALLON (3.8 L)

SYRUP + SELTZER

¼ cup (40 g) 40L caramel malt

1 cup (235 ml) water

2¼ cups (450 g) sugar

2 tablespoons (28 ml) pure vanilla extract

1 teaspoon pure almond extract

(syrup for 1 gallon [3.8 L] finished soda; use 2 to 3 tablespoons [28 to 45 ml] per 8 ounces [235 ml] carbonated water, or to taste)

STRAIGHT CARBONATION

¼ cup (40 g) 40L caramel malt

15 cups (3.5 L) water

2¼ cups (450 g) sugar

2 tablespoons (28 ml) pure vanilla extract

1 teaspoon pure almond extract

FERMENTATION

¼ cup (40 g) 40L caramel malt

15 cups (3.5 L) water

2½ cups (500 g) sugar

2½ tablespoons (12.5 ml) pure vanilla extract

1 teaspoon pure almond extract

⅛ teaspoon Champagne yeast

0.5 g yeast nutrient

SYRUP + SELTZER

2 cups (475 ml) water

18 to 24 spruce tips (30 g)

2 cups (400 g) sugar

2 tablespoons (40 g) molasses

¼ teaspoon citric acid

(syrup for 1 gallon [3.8 L] finished soda; use 2 to 4 tablespoons [28 to 60 ml] per 8 ounces [235 ml] carbonated water, or to taste)

STRAIGHT CARBONATION

15 cups (3.5 L) water

18 to 24 spruce tips (30 g)

2 cups (400 g) sugar

2 tablespoons (40 g) molasses

¼ teaspoon citric acid

FERMENTATION

15 cups (3.5 L) water

25 to 30 spruce tips (40 g)

2¼ cups (450 g) sugar

2 tablespoons (40 g) molasses

¼ teaspoon citric acid

⅛ teaspoon Champagne yeast

1 g yeast nutrient

Spruce tips are the bright green new growth on the boughs of a spruce tree and can be clipped in the spring. They were occasionally used in beer making in certain parts of the world and served the same purpose that hops do today. Spruce beer as a soft drink is also available in some parts of Canada. Some people can be extra sensitive to spruce and swear that it tastes like pine-scented cleaner. Go easy the first time trying it. I think that it smells of Christmas trees, and as such I included it among the holiday recipes. With harvest in the spring, the tips will have to be frozen for use during the holidays, so it takes some planning. For more holiday flavor, try adding some warming spices like ginger and cinnamon.

SPRUCE BEER

In a saucepan, combine the water and spruce tips and bring to a boil. Remove from the heat. For the syrup and seltzer method, use 2 cups (475 ml) water; otherwise, use as much water as is practical to strain. Let steep for 30 to 60 minutes. Strain out the spruce tips and return the water to the saucepan. Add the sugar, molasses, and citric acid and heat over medium-high heat until the sugar has dissolved.

FOR THE SYRUP AND SELTZER METHOD Chill the syrup and add to carbonated water.

FOR STRAIGHT CARBONATION OR FERMENTATION Add the rest of the water to the syrup.

FOR STRAIGHT CARBONATION Chill the mixture before adding it to the keg or carbonator of your choice.

FOR FERMENTATION Hydrate the yeast in ¼ cup (60 ml) or less of warm water. Add the hydrated yeast to the mixture after it has cooled to 10 to 15°F (5.5 to 8°C) above room temperature. Stir in the yeast nutrient. Mix well and then bottle.

YIELD 1 GALLON (3.8 L)

SYRUP + SELTZER

¼ cup (40 g) 20L or 40L caramel malt

1 cup (235 ml) water

1 teaspoon ground cinnamon

1 cup (200 g) granulated sugar

1 cup (225 g) lightly packed light brown sugar

¾ cup (175 ml) apple juice concentrate

¼ teaspoon butter flavoring

(syrup for 1 gallon [3.8 L] finished soda; use 2½ to 4 tablespoons [40 to 60 ml] per 8 ounces [235 ml] carbonated water, or to taste)

STRAIGHT CARBONATION

¼ cup (40 g) 20L or 40L caramel malt

14½ cups (3.4 L) water

1 teaspoon ground cinnamon

1 cup (200 g) granulated sugar

1 cup (225 g) lightly packed light brown sugar

¾ cup (175 ml) apple juice concentrate

¼ teaspoon butter flavoring

FERMENTATION

¼ cup (40 g) 20L or 40L caramel malt

12½ (2.9 L) cups water

1 teaspoon ground cinnamon

1 cup (200 g) granulated sugar

1 cup (225 g) lightly packed light brown sugar

3 cups (700 ml) 100% apple juice

¼ teaspoon butter flavoring

⅛ teaspoon Champagne yeast

1 g yeast nutrient

Tangy apple with warm cinnamon alongside notes of caramel and butter flavors make this soda taste like the classic dessert. The butter flavor and caramel malt can certainly be omitted for an easier and less complex apple-cinnamon soda, but they add the finishing touches for a nostalgic, holiday flavor.

APPLE PIE

Using a grain mill, crack the caramel malt. In a saucepan, combine the water and cinnamon, bring to a boil, and then remove from the heat. For the syrup and seltzer method, use 1 cup (235 ml) water; otherwise, use as much water as is practical to strain. Add the crushed grain and let steep for 20 to 30 minutes. Strain out the grain and spice and return the water to the saucepan. Add the sugars and heat over medium-high heat until the sugar has dissolved. Remove from the heat and add the juice concentrate.

FOR THE SYRUP AND SELTZER METHOD Chill the syrup, add the butter flavoring, and add to carbonated water.

FOR STRAIGHT CARBONATION OR FERMENTATION Add the rest of the water and the butter flavoring to the syrup.

FOR STRAIGHT CARBONATION Chill the mixture before adding it to the keg or carbonator of your choice.

FOR FERMENTATION Hydrate the yeast in ¼ cup (60 ml) or less of warm water. Add the hydrated yeast to the mixture after it has cooled to 10 to 15°F (5.5 to 8°C) above room temperature. Stir in the yeast nutrient. Mix well and then bottle.

YIELD 1 GALLON (3.8 L)

One autumn while cruising through a golden-arched drive-through, I noticed that they had a limited-time-offer shake that had an ambiguous name like "harvest" or "autumn." I thought it sounded mildly interesting, so I ordered one. It turned out to be amazing! It tasted like pumpkin pie and apple pie all blended up with vanilla ice cream. But at the same time, it was so much more. Somehow it evoked memories of brightly colored falling leaves, backyard football games, back-to-school carnivals, and anticipation of Halloween. Well played, mega-corporation product developers, well played. I tried to capture the same feelings and flavors with this soda. I may not have done as well as they did, but the addition of vanilla ice cream will certainly go a long way ... excuse me while I grab a soda and dig through the freezer for some ice cream.

HARVEST APPLE

In a saucepan, combine the water, cloves, ginger paste, and cinnamon, bring to a boil, and then remove from the heat. For the syrup and seltzer method, use 1 cup (235 ml) water; otherwise, use it all. Let steep for 30 minutes, strain out the spices and return the water to the saucepan. Add the sugar, the juice concentrate or juice, and the purée and heat over medium-high heat until the sugar has dissolved.

FOR THE SYRUP AND SELTZER METHOD Chill the syrup and add to carbonated water.

FOR STRAIGHT CARBONATION Chill the mixture before adding it to the keg or carbonator of your choice.

FOR FERMENTATION Hydrate the yeast in ¼ cup (60 ml) or less of warm water. Add the hydrated yeast to the mixture after it has cooled to 10 to 15°F (5.5 to 8°C) above room temperature. Stir in the yeast nutrient. Mix well and then bottle.

YIELD 1 GALLON (3.8 L)

SYRUP + SELTZER

1 cup (235 ml) water

6 to 8 whole cloves

½ teaspoon ginger paste

1½ teaspoons ground cinnamon

2 cups (400 g) sugar

1 cup (235 ml) apple juice concentrate

3 tablespoons (46 g) pumpkin purée

(syrup for 1 gallon [3.8 L] finished soda; use 2½ to 4 tablespoons [40 to 60 ml] per 8 ounces [235 ml] carbonated water, or to taste)

STRAIGHT CARBONATION

13 cups (3.1 L) water

6 to 8 whole cloves

½ teaspoon ginger paste

1½ teaspoons ground cinnamon

2 cups (400 g) sugar

1 cup (235 ml) apple juice concentrate

3 tablespoons (46 g) pumpkin purée

FERMENTATION

10 cups (2.4 L) water

8 to 10 whole cloves

1 teaspoon ginger paste

1½ teaspoons ground cinnamon

2¼ cups (450 g) sugar

4 cups (950 ml) 100% apple juice

¼ cup (46 g) pumpkin purée

⅛ teaspoon Champagne yeast

1 g yeast nutrient

SYRUP + SELTZER

1 cup (235 ml) water

2 cups (450 g) lightly packed light brown sugar

¾ cup (175 ml) apple juice concentrate

½ cup (120 ml) orange juice concentrate

¼ cup (60 ml) fresh lemon juice

Spice Blend (opposite) or 1 cinnamon-spice herbal tea bag

(syrup for 1 gallon [3.8 L] finished soda; use 3 to 4 tablespoons [45 to 60 ml] per 8 ounces [235 ml] carbonated water, or to taste)

STRAIGHT CARBONATION

13½ cups (3.2 L) water

2 cups (450 g) lightly packed light brown sugar

¾ cup (175 ml) apple juice concentrate

½ cup (120 ml) orange juice concentrate

¼ cup (60 ml) fresh lemon juice

Spice Blend (opposite) or 1 cinnamon-spice herbal tea bag

Wassail is usually a warm mulled cider drink. Apple juice, orange juice, and lemon juice make up the fruit base, while the ginger, nutmeg, cloves, and cinnamon make up the spices. A good cinnamon-spiced herbal tea mix also makes a good substitute for the spices, with no straining. If going a-wassailing during the holidays, the mixture likely should be served warm and still. With added carbonation, it makes for a lovely holiday soda served cold and fizzy.

WASSAIL

In a saucepan, combine the water, cloves, cinnamon, ginger, and nutmeg, bring to a boil, and then remove from the heat. For the syrup and seltzer method, use 1 cup (235 ml) water; otherwise, use it all. Let steep for 20 to 30 minutes. Strain out the spices and return the water to the saucepan. Add the sugar and heat until it has dissolved. Remove from the heat and allow the syrup or mixture to cool. Add the juice concentrates and juice.

FOR THE SYRUP AND SELTZER METHOD Chill the syrup and add to carbonated water.

FOR STRAIGHT CARBONATION Chill the mixture before adding it to the keg or carbonator of your choice.

FOR FERMENTATION Hydrate the yeast in ¼ cup (60 ml) or less of warm water. Add the hydrated yeast to the mixture after it has cooled to 10 to 15°F (5.5 to 8°C) above room temperature. Stir in the yeast nutrient. Mix well and then bottle.

YIELD 1 GALLON (3.8 L)

FERMENTATION

13½ cups (3.2 L) water

2¼ cups (510 g) lightly packed light brown sugar

¾ cup (175 ml) apple juice concentrate

½ cup (120 ml) orange juice concentrate

¼ cup (60 ml) fresh lemon juice

Spice Blend (below) or 1 cinnamon-spice herbal tea bag

⅛ teaspoon Champagne yeast

0.5 g yeast nutrient

SPICE BLEND

5 to 10 whole cloves

¼ teaspoon ground cinnamon

¼ teaspoon ground ginger

¼ teaspoon ground nutmeg

SYRUP + SELTZER

1 cup (235 ml) water

1 cinnamon-spice herbal tea bag

2 cups (400 g) sugar

½ cup (120 ml) apple juice concentrate

¾ cup (175 ml) cranberry juice concentrate

(syrup for 1 gallon [3.8 L] finished soda; use 3 to 5 tablespoons [45 to 75 ml] per 8 ounces [235 ml] carbonated water, or to taste)

STRAIGHT CARBONATION

13 cups (3.1 L) water

1 cinnamon-spice herbal tea bag

2 cups (400 g) sugar

½ cup (120 ml) apple juice concentrate

¾ cup (175 ml) cranberry juice concentrate or 6 cups (1.4 L) 100% cranberry juice blend

FERMENTATION

13 cups (3.1 L) water

1 cinnamon-spice herbal tea bag

2¼ cups (450 g) sugar

½ cup (120 ml) apple juice concentrate

¾ cup (175 ml) cranberry juice concentrate or 6 cups (1.4 L) 100% cranberry juice blend

⅛ teaspoon Champagne yeast

0.5 g yeast nutrient

This recipe is a combination of two great holiday flavors: sparkling cider and spiced cranberry. A good source of spice is a cinnamon-spiced herbal tea bag, or use traditional mulling spices. It's hard to find cranberries year-round, so a juice concentrate is a good substitute. Try to find one that is 100% juice instead of a sweetened juice drink. Pure cranberry juice is rarely sold, but there are some cranberry blends that are 100% juice.

SPICED CRANBERRY

In a saucepan, combine the water and tea bag, bring to a boil, and then remove from the heat. For the syrup and seltzer method, use 1 cup (235 ml) water; otherwise, use it all. Let steep for 20 to 30 minutes. Remove the tea bag. Add the sugar and heat until it has dissolved. Remove from the heat, allow the syrup or mixture to cool, and then add the juice concentrate or juice.

FOR THE SYRUP AND SELTZER METHOD Chill the syrup and add to carbonated water.

FOR STRAIGHT CARBONATION Chill the mixture before adding it to the keg or carbonator of your choice.

FOR FERMENTATION Hydrate the yeast in ¼ cup (60 ml) or less of warm water. Add the hydrated yeast to the mixture after it has cooled to 10 to 15°F (5.5 to 8°C) above room temperature. Stir in the yeast nutrient. Mix well and then bottle.

YIELD 1 GALLON (3.8 L)

Cinnamon candy is not as common during the holidays as peppermint or chocolate, but something about it reminds me of Christmas. Instead of trying to use other ingredients to mimic the cinnamon candies, I thought that appropriating their flavor would be a more direct approach. This can't necessarily be done with all candies, but hard candies are usually little more than sugar and flavor, which is what goes into a soda syrup anyway.

CINNAMON CANDY

In a saucepan, combine the water, sugar, and candies and heat until dissolved. For the syrup and seltzer method, use 1 cup (235 ml) water; otherwise, use it all.

FOR THE SYRUP AND SELTZER METHOD Chill the syrup and add to carbonated water.

FOR STRAIGHT CARBONATION Chill the mixture before adding it to the keg or carbonator of your choice.

FOR FERMENTATION Hydrate the yeast in ¼ cup (60 ml) or less of warm water. Add the hydrated yeast to the mixture after it has cooled to 10 to 15°F (5.5 to 8°C) above room temperature. Stir in the yeast nutrient. Mix well and then bottle.

YIELD 1 GALLON (3.8 L)

RECIPE VARIANT

For use with other hard candies, avoid any candies with starch or pectin ingredients. Any candy that has a robust flavor and few extra ingredients should substitute well.

SYRUP + SELTZER

1 cup (235 ml) water

1 cup (200 g) sugar

1 cup (150 g) cinnamon imperials

(syrup for 1 gallon [3.8 L] finished soda; use 1½ to 2 tablespoons [25 to 28 ml] per 8 ounces [235 ml] carbonated water, or to taste)

STRAIGHT CARBONATION

15 cups (3.5 L) water

1 cup (200 g) sugar

1 cup (150 g) cinnamon imperials

FERMENTATION

15 cups (3.5 L) water

1¼ cups (250 g) sugar

1 cup (150 g) cinnamon imperials

⅛ teaspoon Champagne yeast

1.5 g yeast nutrient

This holiday-inspired soda draws its main flavors from ginger, molasses, and caramel malt. This soda is a reminder that gingerbread flavor is good for more than just decorative little men and candy-covered houses. A darker caramel malt is suitable for this recipe and blends well with the molasses. It may not sprout legs and taunt anyone into chasing it, but it does go fast.

GINGERBREAD

Using a grain mill, crack the caramel malt. In a saucepan, combine the water, ginger, cinnamon, and cloves, bring to a boil, and then remove from the heat. For the syrup and seltzer method, use 1 cup (235 ml) water; otherwise, use as much water as is practical to strain. Add the crushed grain and let steep for 20 minutes. Strain out the grain and spices and return the water to the saucepan. Add the sugar and molasses and then heat over medium-high heat until the sugar has dissolved.

FOR THE SYRUP AND SELTZER METHOD Chill the syrup and add to carbonated water.

FOR STRAIGHT CARBONATION OR FERMENTATION Add the rest of the water to the syrup.

FOR STRAIGHT CARBONATION Chill the mixture before adding it to the keg or carbonator of your choice.

FOR FERMENTATION Hydrate the yeast in ¼ cup (60 ml) or less of warm water. Add the hydrated yeast to the mixture after it has cooled to 10 to 15°F (5.5 to 8°C) above room temperature. Stir in the yeast nutrient. Mix well and then bottle.

YIELD 1 GALLON (3.8 L)

SYRUP + SELTZER

¼ cup (40 g) 60L caramel malt

1 cup (235 ml) water

1 teaspoon ground ginger

1 teaspoon ground cinnamon

¼ teaspoon ground cloves

2 cups granulated (400 g) or brown (450 g) sugar

2 tablespoons (40 g) molasses

(syrup for 1 gallon [3.8 L] finished soda; use 1½ to 2 tablespoons [25 to 28 ml] per 8 ounces [235 ml] carbonated water, or to taste)

STRAIGHT CARBONATION

¼ cup (40 g) 60L caramel malt

15 cups (3.5 L) water

1 teaspoon ground ginger

1 teaspoon ground cinnamon

¼ teaspoon ground cloves

2 cups white (400 g) or brown (450 g) sugar

2 tablespoons (40 g) molasses

FERMENTATION

⅓ cup (54 g) 60L caramel malt

15 cups (3.5 L) water

1½ teaspoons ground ginger

1 teaspoon ground cinnamon

¼ teaspoon ground cloves

2 cups white (400 g) or brown (450 g) sugar

2 tablespoons (40 g) molasses

⅛ teaspoon Champagne yeast

0.5 g yeast nutrient

SYRUP + SELTZER

½ cup (120 ml) water

1 (2-inch, or 5 cm) piece fresh ginger, sliced

1 cup (200 g) sugar

1 cup (235 ml) white grape juice concentrate

1 cup (235 ml) apple juice concentrate

2 tablespoons (28 ml) fresh lemon juice

(syrup for 1 gallon [3.8 L] finished soda; use 2 to 4 tablespoons [28 to 60 ml] per 8 ounces [235 ml] carbonated water, or to taste)

STRAIGHT CARBONATION

7½ cups (1.8 L) water

1 (2-inch, or 5 cm) piece fresh ginger, sliced

1 cup (200 g) sugar

4 cups (950 ml) 100% white grape juice

4 cups (950 ml) 100% apple juice

2 tablespoons (28 ml) fresh lemon juice

FERMENTATION

7½ cups (1.8 L) water

1 (2-inch, or 5 cm) piece fresh ginger, sliced

1¼ cups (250 g) sugar

4 cups (950 ml) 100% white grape juice

4 cups (950 ml) 100% apple juice

2 tablespoons (28 ml) fresh lemon juice

⅛ teaspoon Champagne yeast

1 g yeast nutrient

This is an adaptation of a recipe that my aunt served at a family Thanksgiving that was basically a mix of apple juice, white grape juice, and ginger ale. While it's probably not a dead match for real Champagne, it does have a more sophisticated taste than a plain sparkling juice. This would be more than welcome at any teetotaler's New Year's party.

FAUX CHAMPAGNE

In a saucepan, combine the water and ginger, bring to a boil, and then remove from the heat. For the syrup and seltzer method, use ½ cup (120 ml) water; otherwise, use it all. Let steep for 30 minutes, strain out the ginger, and return the water to the saucepan. Add the sugar, juices concentrates, and juices and then heat over medium-high heat until the sugar has dissolved.

FOR THE SYRUP AND SELTZER METHOD Chill the syrup and add to carbonated water.

FOR STRAIGHT CARBONATION Chill the mixture before adding it to the keg or carbonator of your choice.

FOR FERMENTATION Hydrate the yeast in ¼ cup (60 ml) or less of warm water. Add the hydrated yeast to the mixture after it has cooled to 10 to 15°F (5.5 to 8°C) above room temperature. Stir in the yeast nutrient. Mix well and then bottle.

YIELD 1 GALLON (3.8 L)

There's something about candy canes that conjures up holiday memories a little bit more readily than, say, an everyday peppermint breath mint. Peppermint has long been used as a calming tea and for various other medicinal purposes. Bear in mind that it also is used in toothpaste, which is what this soda will end up tasting like if too much peppermint is used. A little mint certainly can go a long way. For serving during the holidays, split the batch in half and color one half red with food coloring; then bottle it in clear bottles so that you have alternating red and clear beverages lining the table.

CANDY CANE

In a saucepan, combine the sugar and water and heat to dissolve. For the syrup and seltzer method, use 1 cup (235 ml) water; otherwise, use it all. If using tea bags, steep them in the water to the desired strength before adding the sugar. Remove from the heat and let the syrup or mixture cool. Add the extract, if using.

FOR THE SYRUP AND SELTZER METHOD Chill the syrup and add to carbonated water.

FOR STRAIGHT CARBONATION Chill the mixture before adding it to the keg or carbonator of your choice.

FOR FERMENTATION Hydrate the yeast in ¼ cup (60 ml) or less of warm water. Add the hydrated yeast to the mixture after it has cooled to 10 to 15°F (5.5 to 8°C) above room temperature. Stir in the yeast nutrient. Mix well and then bottle.

YIELD 1 GALLON (3.8 L)

SYRUP + SELTZER

2 cups (400 g) sugar

1 cup (235 ml) water

½ teaspoon pure peppermint extract or 1 peppermint herbal tea bag

(syrup for 1 gallon [3.8 L] finished soda; use 1½ to 2 tablespoons [25 to 28 ml] per 8 ounces [235 ml] carbonated water, or to taste)

STRAIGHT CARBONATION

2 cups (400 g) sugar

15 cups (3.5 L) water

½ teaspoon pure peppermint extract or 1 peppermint herbal tea bag

FERMENTATION

2¼ cups (450 g) sugar

15 cups (3.5 L) water

½ teaspoon pure peppermint extract or 1 peppermint herbal tea bag

⅛ teaspoon Champagne yeast

1 g yeast nutrient

SYRUP + SELTZER

2 cups (450 ml) water

½ cup (88 g) dried plums (prunes)

½ teaspoon ground cardamom

4 sections star anise

2 cups (400 g) sugar

1 tablespoon (15 ml) pure almond extract

1 teaspoon vanilla extract

(syrup for 1 gallon [3.8 L] finished soda; use 2 to 4 tablespoons [28 to 60 ml] per 8 ounces [235 ml] carbonated water, or to taste)

STRAIGHT CARBONATION

15 cups (3.5 L) water

½ cup (88 g) dried plums (prunes)

½ teaspoon ground cardamom

4 sections star anise

2 cups (400 g) sugar

1 tablespoon (15 ml) pure almond extract

1 teaspoon vanilla extract

FERMENTATION

15 cups (3.5 L) water

⅔ cup (117 g) dried plums (prunes)

½ teaspoon ground cardamom

4 sections star anise

2¼ cups (450 g) sugar

1 tablespoon (15 ml) pure almond extract

1 teaspoon vanilla extract

⅛ teaspoon Champagne yeast

1 g yeast nutrient

Thanks to an early American poem that largely shaped the country's Christmas traditions, many have heard of sugarplums. However, I'd wager few have tasted them, let alone had them dance in their heads. I hope this recipe will change that at least somewhat. I normally like to use pure vanilla extracts in my recipes, but this works with any vanilla extract.

SUGARPLUM

In a saucepan, combine the water, plums, cardamom, and anise, bring to a boil, and then remove from the heat. For the syrup and seltzer method, use 2 cups (475 ml) water; otherwise, use as much water as is practical to strain. Let steep for 20 to 30 minutes, strain out the fruit and spices, and return the water to the saucepan. Add the sugar and heat over medium-high heat until the sugar has dissolved.

FOR THE SYRUP AND SELTZER METHOD Chill the syrup, add the extracts, and add to carbonated water.

FOR STRAIGHT CARBONATION OR FERMENTATION Add the rest of the water and extracts.

FOR STRAIGHT CARBONATION Chill the mixture before adding it to the keg or carbonator of your choice.

FOR FERMENTATION Hydrate the yeast in ¼ cup (60 ml) or less of warm water. Add the hydrated yeast to the mixture after it has cooled to 10 to 15°F (5.5 to 8°C) above room temperature. Stir in the yeast nutrient. Mix well and then bottle.

YIELD 1 GALLON (3.8 L)

What goes better with apples than caramel? Cinnamon may make the list, but I'd guess that's about it. To transform apples and caramel into bubbly liquid form is surprisingly easy, and the result is just as tasty. Caramelizing sugar is easy to do, but it's also easy to take it too far and end up with burnt sugar. I find that adding water before it seems dark enough is usually just right because it does seem to get a little bit darker even after that point.

CARAMEL APPLE

In a saucepan, heat the sugar over medium heat. Stir constantly so that it heats and melts evenly and be careful that it doesn't burn. When the sugar has turned a deep yellow to amber color, carefully add 1½ cups (355 ml) of the water. Stir to combine. Let the syrup cool and then add the juice concentrate or juice, vanilla, and citric acid.

FOR THE SYRUP AND SELTZER METHOD Chill the syrup and add to carbonated water.

FOR STRAIGHT CARBONATION OR FERMENTATION Add the rest of the water.

FOR STRAIGHT CARBONATION Chill the mixture before adding it to the keg or carbonator of your choice.

FOR FERMENTATION Hydrate the yeast in ¼ cup (60 ml) or less of warm water. Add the hydrated yeast to the mixture after it has cooled to 10 to 15°F (5.5 to 8°C) above room temperature. Stir in the yeast nutrient. Mix well and then bottle.

YIELD 1 GALLON (3.8 L)

SYRUP + SELTZER

2¼ cups (450 g) sugar

1½ cups (355 ml) water

1 cup (235 ml) apple juice concentrate

½ teaspoon pure vanilla extract

¼ teaspoon citric acid

(syrup for 1 gallon [3.8 L] finished soda; use 3 to 4 tablespoons [45 to 60 ml] per 8 ounces [235 ml] carbonated water, or to taste)

STRAIGHT CARBONATION

2¼ cups (450 g) sugar

14 cups (3.3 L) water

1 cup (235 ml) apple juice concentrate or 4 cups (950 ml) 100% apple juice

½ teaspoon pure vanilla extract

¼ teaspoon citric acid

FERMENTATION

2¼ cups (450 g) sugar

13½ cups (3.2 L) water

1¼ cups (285 ml) apple juice concentrate or 5 cups (1.2 L) 100% apple juice

½ teaspoon pure vanilla extract

¼ teaspoon citric acid

⅛ teaspoon Champagne yeast

1 g yeast nutrient

Beyond
the Basics:
Experimental
Sodas

When I worked in a restaurant, one of the main things that we had to prep were green bell peppers. A couple of us were discussing beverage making, and since there was a fair amount of green pepper juice in the bottom of the bin of sliced peppers, we thought it would be an interesting mix with a lemon-lime soda. Initially it was intended as a joke, but it turned out that it wasn't half bad. This recipe comes from that off-the-wall "what-if," but it's had some refinement since then.

GREEN PEPPER

In a saucepan, combine the peppers, lemon zest, and water. For the syrup and seltzer method, use 2 cups (475 ml) water; otherwise, use as much water as is practical to strain. Bring to a boil and then remove from the heat and let steep for 20 minutes. Strain out the peppers and zest and then return the water to the saucepan. Add the sugar and lemon juice and heat until the sugar has dissolved.

FOR THE SYRUP AND SELTZER METHOD Chill the syrup and add to carbonated water.

FOR STRAIGHT CARBONATION OR FERMENTATION Add the rest of the water to the strained syrup.

FOR STRAIGHT CARBONATION Chill the mixture before adding it to the keg or carbonator of your choice.

FOR FERMENTATION Hydrate the yeast in ¼ cup (60 ml) or less of warm water. Add the hydrated yeast to the mixture after it has cooled to 10 to 15°F (5.5 to 8°C) above room temperature. Stir in the yeast nutrient. Mix well and then bottle.

YIELD 1 GALLON (3.8 L)

SYRUP + SELTZER

2 large green bell peppers, cut into strips

Zest and juice of 1 lemon

2 cups (475 ml) water

2 cups (400 g) sugar

(syrup for 1 gallon [3.8 L] finished soda; use 2½ to 4 tablespoons [40 to 60 ml] per 8 ounces [235 ml] carbonated water, or to taste)

STRAIGHT CARBONATION

2 large green bell peppers, cut into strips

Zest and juice of 1 lemon

15 cups (3.5 L) water

2 cups (400 g) sugar

FERMENTATION

2 large green bell peppers, cut into strips

Zest and juice of 1 lemon

15 cups (3.5 L) water

2¼ cups (450 g) sugar

⅛ teaspoon Champagne yeast

1 g yeast nutrient

SYRUP + SELTZER

½ cup (120 ml) water

1¾ cups (175 g) sugar

½ cup (120 ml) fresh
lemon juice

1½ cups (355 ml) orange
juice concentrate

1¼ cups (285 ml) 100% carrot
juice

(syrup for 1 gallon [3.8 L]
finished soda; use 3 to 4
tablespoons [30 to 60 ml] per
8 ounces [235 ml] carbonated
water, or to taste)

STRAIGHT CARBONATION

12½ cups (2.9 L) water

1¾ cups (175 g) sugar

½ cup (120 ml) fresh
lemon juice

1½ cups (355 ml) orange juice
concentrate or 6 cups (1.4 L)
100% orange juice

1¼ cups (285 ml) 100% carrot
juice

FERMENTATION

12½ cups (2.9 L) water

2 cups (400 g) sugar

½ cup (60 ml) fresh
lemon juice

1½ cups (355 ml) orange juice
concentrate or 6 cups (1.4 L)
100% orange juice

1¼ cups (285 ml) 100%
carrot juice

⅛ teaspoon Champagne yeast

0.5 g yeast nutrient

In the supermarkets of Europe, A.C.E. juice can be found in many places. It is named such for the vitamins that it is fortified with. The A and C I can understand, but not many fruits are particularly high in vitamin E, so I'm not sure how it got there other than fortification. I can't guarantee the vitamin content of vitamin E in this recipe, or any of the vitamins, for that matter. What I like most about this is how the carrot softens the sharp sourness of the two citrus juices. And who doesn't need a little more carrot in their diet? This one is my favorite fermented soda because it is so fast and tastes so clean.

A.C.E.

In a saucepan, combine ½ cup (120 ml) of the water, sugar, and half of the lemon juice. Bring to a boil and then let it simmer for about 5 minutes. Remove from the heat and let cool. Add the rest of the juices and/or concentrate.

FOR THE SYRUP AND SELTZER METHOD Chill the syrup and add to carbonated water.

FOR STRAIGHT CARBONATION OR FERMENTATION Add the rest of the water.

FOR STRAIGHT CARBONATION Chill the mixture before adding it to the keg or carbonator of your choice.

FOR FERMENTATION Hydrate the yeast in ¼ cup (60 ml) or less of warm water. Add the hydrated yeast to the mixture after it has cooled to 10 to 15°F (5.5 to 8°C) above room temperature. Stir in the yeast nutrient. Mix well and then bottle.

YIELD 1 GALLON (3.8 L)

Celery soda has long been a feature of kosher delis. The brand that produced it was at one time the only line of kosher sodas available. Its taste is herbal and characteristic of celery, but surprisingly refreshing. There are some recipes floating around that use the stalks put through a juicer, but the flavor is also fine with the easier-to-handle seeds. Cardamom blends well with the celery flavor to bring it back to something that tastes like it belongs more in a soda than a chicken soup.

CELERY

In a saucepan, combine the 1 cup (235 ml) of the water, celery seed, and cardamom, bring to a boil, and then remove from the heat. Let steep for 20 minutes. Strain out the spices and then return the water to the saucepan. Add the sugar and heat until it has dissolved.

FOR THE SYRUP AND SELTZER METHOD Chill the syrup and add to carbonated water.

FOR STRAIGHT CARBONATION OR FERMENTATION Add the rest of the water to the syrup.

FOR STRAIGHT CARBONATION Chill the mixture before adding it to the keg or carbonator of your choice.

FOR FERMENTATION Hydrate the yeast in ¼ cup (60 ml) or less of warm water. Add the hydrated yeast to the mixture after it has cooled to 10 to 15°F (5.5 to 8°C) above room temperature. Stir in the yeast nutrient. Mix well and then bottle.

YIELD 1 GALLON (3.8 L)

SYRUP + SELTZER

1 cup (235 ml) water

3 tablespoons (20 g) celery seed

½ teaspoon ground cardamom

2 cups (400 g) sugar

(syrup for 1 gallon [3.8 L] finished soda; use 1½ to 2 tablespoons [25 to 28 ml] per 8 ounces [235 ml] carbonated water, or to taste)

STRAIGHT CARBONATION

15 cups (3.5 L) water

3 tablespoons (20 g) celery seed

½ teaspoon ground cardamom

2 cups (400 g) sugar

FERMENTATION

15 cups (3.5 L) water

3 tablespoons (20 g) celery seed

½ teaspoon ground cardamom

2¼ cups (450 g) sugar

⅛ teaspoon Champagne yeast

1 g yeast nutrient

SYRUP + SELTZER

1 cup (235 ml) water

Zest of 2 lemons

3 tablespoons (15 g) whole black peppercorns

2 cups (400 g) sugar

2 tablespoons (28 ml) fresh lemon juice

(syrup for 1 gallon [3.8 L] finished soda; use 1½ to 2½ tablespoons [25 to 40 ml] per 8 ounces [235 ml] carbonated water, or to taste)

STRAIGHT CARBONATION

15 cups (3.5 L) water

Zest of 2 lemons

3 tablespoons (15 g) whole black peppercorns

2 cups (400 g) sugar

2 tablespoons (28 ml) fresh lemon juice

FERMENTATION

15 cups (3.5 L) water

Zest of 2 lemons

3 tablespoons (15 g) whole black peppercorns

2¼ cups (450 g) sugar

2 tablespoons (28 ml) fresh lemon juice

⅛ teaspoon Champagne yeast

1 g yeast nutrient

Lemon and pepper go together and work well with just about every-thing from chicken and fish to rice to . . . soda? Steeping the pepper-corns does not bring the level of heat that black pepper usually has when added to foods as a whole or ground spice. The pepper flavor here is not too far from nutmeg, and together with the lemon makes a spicier lemonade, similar to a ginger ale without the bite.

LEMON PEPPERCORN

In a saucepan, combine the water, zest, and peppercorns. For the syrup and seltzer method, use 1 cup (235 ml) water; otherwise, use as much water as is practical to strain. Bring to a boil and then remove from the heat and let steep for 20 to 30 minutes. Strain out the zest and peppercorns and then return the water to the saucepan. Add the sugar and heat until it has dissolved. Remove the syrup from the heat and add the lemon juice.

FOR THE SYRUP AND SELTZER METHOD Chill the syrup and add to carbonated water.

FOR STRAIGHT CARBONATION OR FERMENTATION Add the rest of the water to the strained syrup.

FOR STRAIGHT CARBONATION Chill the mixture before adding it to the keg or carbonator of your choice.

FOR FERMENTATION Hydrate the yeast in ¼ cup (60 ml) or less of warm water. Add the hydrated yeast to the mixture after it has cooled to 10 to 15°F (5.5 to 8°C) above room temperature. Stir in the yeast nutrient. Mix well and then bottle.

YIELD 1 GALLON (3.8 L)

Sodas are usually cold and refreshing instead of hot and spicy. It surprises most people that spice in a soda can be refreshing and welcome. Lime and jalapeño blend well in this spiced-up soda. The jalapeño flavor comes through with the tart of the lime and the sweetness of the sugar, but the heat is a delayed tingle. This is another soda that ferments very cleanly without much yeast flavor. I removed the seeds from one of the jalapeños to lessen the heat, but that's not necessary for those who like a lot of kick. The lime juice from the zested limes wasn't quite enough to get ½ cup (120 ml), so it may be necessary to supplement with more squeezed limes or bottled lime juice.

CHILE LIME

In a saucepan, combine 2 cups (475 ml) of the water, jalapeños, and lime zest. Bring to a boil and then simmer for 2 to 3 minutes. Remove from the heat and let steep for 20 to 30 minutes. Strain out the zest and jalapeños and return the water to the saucepan. Add the sugar and the juices and heat until the sugar has dissolved.

FOR THE SYRUP AND SELTZER METHOD Chill the syrup and add to carbonated water.

FOR STRAIGHT CARBONATION OR FERMENTATION Add the rest of the water.

FOR STRAIGHT CARBONATION Chill the mixture before adding it to the keg or carbonator of your choice.

FOR FERMENTATION Hydrate the yeast in ¼ cup (60 ml) or less of warm water. Add the hydrated yeast to the mixture after it has cooled to 10 to 15°F (5.5 to 8°C) above room temperature. Stir in the yeast nutrient. Mix well and then bottle.

YIELD 1 GALLON (3.8 L)

SYRUP + SELTZER

2 cups (475 ml) water

2 medium jalapeños (Remove the seeds from 1 chile.)

Zest of 2 limes

2 cups (400 g) sugar

½ cup (120 ml) fresh lime juice

¼ cup (60 ml) fresh lemon juice

(syrup for 1 gallon [3.8 L] finished soda; use 3 to 4½ tablespoons [45 to 70 ml] per 8 ounces [235 ml] carbonated water, or to taste)

STRAIGHT CARBONATION

14½ cups (3.4 L) water

2 medium jalapeños (Remove the seeds from 1 chile.)

Zest of 2 limes

2 cups (400 g) sugar

½ cup (120 ml) fresh lime juice

¼ cup (60 ml) fresh lemon juice

FERMENTATION

15 cups (3.5 L) water

2 medium jalapeños (Remove the seeds from 1 chile.)

Zest of 2 limes

2¼ cups (450 g) sugar

½ cup (120 ml) fresh lime juice

¼ cup (60 ml) fresh lemon juice

⅛ teaspoon Champagne yeast

0.5 g yeast nutrient

SYRUP + SELTZER

4 cups (950 ml) water

2 medium-large sweet potatoes, shredded

½ cup (120 ml) fresh lemon juice

2 cups (400 g) sugar

2 teaspoons ground cinnamon

1 teaspoon ground nutmeg

½ teaspoon ground ginger

(syrup for 1 gallon [3.8 L] finished soda; use 3 to 4 tablespoons [45 to 60 ml] per 8 ounces [235 ml] carbonated water, or to taste)

STRAIGHT CARBONATION

14½ cups (3.4 L) water

2 medium-large sweet potatoes, shredded

½ cup (120 ml) fresh lemon juice

2 cups (400 g) sugar

2 teaspoons ground cinnamon

1 teaspoon ground nutmeg

½ teaspoon ground ginger

FERMENTATION

14½ cups (3.5 L) water

2 medium-large sweet potatoes, shredded

Zest and juice of 1 lemon

2½ cups (450 g) sugar

2 teaspoons ground cinnamon

1 teaspoon ground nutmeg

½ teaspoon ground ginger

⅛ teaspoon Champagne yeast

0.5 g yeast nutrient

This is an adaptation of a recipe called sweet potato fly from Sandor Katz. His book deals with fermentation of just about everything. I highly recommend it to anyone who wants to delve deeper into fermentation. His recipe uses whey as a starter for lacto fermentation, which is a bacterial fermentation similar to that used for making yogurt, instead of a yeast fermentation. That has not been an area where I've chosen to focus, so this recipe is partly a reminder that there are other options for fermentation than what I present. The result is somewhat reminiscent of sweet potato pie and lemonade blended together.

SWEET POTATO

For all three carbonation methods, combine all of the ingredients in a saucepan, holding back half the lemon juice, and bring to a boil. (If using the fermentation method, leave out the yeast and yeast nutrient.) Simmer until the liquid is reduced by about half and then remove from the heat. Strain out the solids, pressing them to extract all the syrup. Let cool to about room temperature and then add the remaining lemon juice.

FOR THE SYRUP AND SELTZER METHOD Chill the syrup and add to carbonated water.

FOR STRAIGHT CARBONATION Chill the mixture before adding it to the keg or carbonator of your choice.

FOR FERMENTATION Hydrate the yeast in ¼ cup (60 ml) or less of warm water. When it begins to bubble, combine all the ingredients and let ferment for 12 to 18 hours. Strain out the solids, pressing to extract all of the liquid. Pour into clean bottles and continue to ferment until the bottles are firm.

YIELD 1 GALLON (3.8 L)

Cucumber and melon is a classic combination that can be found in many different flavored and scented products. The flavors blend well and complement each other nicely. In this version, lime is added to increase the tartness and make the flavor just a little more complex. It can be difficult to remove all the pulp in this preparation, but the soda still comes out quite nicely.

CUCUMBER MELON

In a saucepan, combine the sugar, half the lime juice, and 1 cup (235 ml) of the water. Heat over medium-high heat until boiling and let boil for about 5 minutes. Meanwhile, dice the cucumber and melon and set aside. Remove the syrup from the heat and pour over the cucumber and melon to macerate. Using a potato masher, crush the macerated melon and cucumber to further release their juice. Using a fine-mesh strainer, strain out the fruit pulp and seeds from the syrup as fully as possible.

FOR THE SYRUP AND SELTZER METHOD Add the remaining citrus juices along with the vanilla, chill the syrup, and add to carbonated water.

FOR STRAIGHT CARBONATION OR FERMENTATION Add the rest of the water and citrus juices to the strained syrup along with the vanilla.

FOR STRAIGHT CARBONATION Chill the mixture before adding it to the keg or carbonator of your choice.

FOR FERMENTATION Hydrate the yeast in ¼ cup (60 ml) or less of warm water. Add the hydrated yeast to the mixture after it has cooled to 10 to 15°F (5.5 to 8°C) above room temperature. Stir in the yeast nutrient. Mix well and then bottle.

YIELD 1 GALLON (3.8 L)

SYRUP + SELTZER

2 cups (400 g) sugar

2 tablespoons (28 ml) fresh lime juice

1 cup (235 ml) water

½ of a medium cucumber

2 (1-inch-thick, or 2.5 cm thick) slices honeydew melon

1 tablespoon (15 ml) fresh lemon juice

½ teaspoon vanilla extract

(syrup for 1 gallon [3.8 L] finished soda; use 2½ to 4 tablespoons [40 to 60 ml] per 8 ounces [235 ml] carbonated water, or to taste)

STRAIGHT CARBONATION

2 cups (400 g) sugar

2 tablespoons (28 ml) fresh lime juice

15 cups (3.5 L) water

½ of a medium cucumber

2 (1-inch-thick, or 2.5 cm thick) slices honeydew melon

1 tablespoon (15 ml) fresh lemon juice

½ teaspoon vanilla extract

FERMENTATION

2¼ cups (450 g) sugar

2 tablespoons (28 ml) fresh lime juice

15 cups (3.5 L) water

½ of a medium cucumber

2 (1-inch-thick, or 2.5 cm thick) slices honeydew melon

1 tablespoon (15 ml) fresh lemon juice

½ teaspoon vanilla extract

⅛ teaspoon Champagne yeast

0.5 g yeast nutrient

SYRUP + SELTZER

¼ cup (40 g) smoked malt

1 cup (235 ml) water

¼ cup (40 g) cut and sifted sassafras root bark

12 sections star anise

2 tablespoons (20 g) cut and sifted wild cherry bark

2 cups (400 g) sugar

(syrup for 1 gallon [3.8 L] finished soda; use 1½ to 2 tablespoons [25 to 28 ml] per 8 ounces [235 ml] carbonated water, or to taste)

STRAIGHT CARBONATION

¼ cup (40 g) smoked malt

15 cups (3.5 L) water

¼ cup (40 g) cut and sifted sassafras root bark

12 sections star anise

2 tablespoons (20 g) cut and sifted wild cherry bark

2 cups (400 g) sugar

FERMENTATION

⅓ cup (53 g) smoked malt

15 cups (3.5 L) water

¼ cup (40 g) cut and sifted sassafras root bark

12 sections star anise

2 tablespoons (20 g) cut and sifted wild cherry bark

2¼ cups (450 g) sugar

⅛ teaspoon Champagne yeast

1 g yeast nutrient

Adding caramel malts to root beer brings it somewhat of a caramel character, but there are other specialty malts used in beer brewing as well that are of use. Smoked malts are sometimes used in porters to give a bold, smoky taste. Adding these malts to root beer gives a character not unlike something that was barbecued. It's the perfect summer treat for the outdoors. The smoked character of the malt can fade quickly, so be sure to add that last to get the most out of it.

SMOKED MALT ROOT BEER

Using a grain mill, crack the malt. In a saucepan, combine the water, sassafras, star anise, and cherry bark. For the syrup and seltzer method, use 1 cup (235 ml) water; otherwise, use as much water as is practical to strain. Bring the water to a boil and then remove from the heat. Add the crushed grain and let steep for 20 to 30 minutes. Strain out the roots and grain and return the water to the saucepan. Add the sugar and heat over medium-high heat until the sugar has dissolved.

FOR THE SYRUP AND SELTZER METHOD Chill the syrup and add to carbonated water.

FOR STRAIGHT CARBONATION OR FERMENTATION Add the rest of the water to the syrup.

FOR STRAIGHT CARBONATION Chill the mixture before adding it to the keg or carbonator of your choice.

FOR FERMENTATION Hydrate the yeast in ¼ cup (60 ml) or less of warm water. Add the hydrated yeast to the mixture after it has cooled to 10 to 15°F (5.5 to 8°C) above room temperature. Stir in the yeast nutrient. Mix well and then bottle.

YIELD 1 GALLON (3.8 L)

five

SCIENCE PROJECTS

Sometimes to fully understand some of the scientific principles it helps to have a little hands-on experience. The most straightforward way to get quality hands-on experience without learning from costly mistakes on large batches is to set up some science experiments to illustrate the principles at hand. With the added bonus of having a few fun options for the next school science fair, these experiments are really meant to aid in sharpening anyone's soda-making skills and provide a good metric based on commercial sodas.

Understanding the principles illustrated in the following experiments really goes a long way in troubleshooting a bad batch. Knowing the pressure in a commercial soda helps when it comes to setting the carbonation pressure on a keg. Knowing the different carbonation methods helps in understanding which one is best suited to any individual taste or to best plan for a large batch if making something for a family get-together. Knowing the acid levels gives a better understanding of what flavors work well with carbonation and what's safe to ferment. Understanding flavor extraction and Brix levels both aid in recipe development.

A high school chemistry textbook would be a handy reference for more information on these principles, but it is by no means essential to understanding these simple experiments. I've tried to keep special equipment to a minimum in order to make these accessible to all.

CARBONATION PRESSURE AND VOLUMES

Determining the pressure in a soda bottle is actually about determining how much carbonation is inside. It can be measured in a somewhat roundabout way by measuring the weight of CO_2 that is released as the sample is decarbonated. Carbonation is measured in volumes, which in metric terms turns out to be about 2 grams per liter. So if the volume of the container is known, and the weight of CO_2 can be measured, then the volumes of CO_2 can be calculated. It's difficult to be precise, but a close approximation works just fine. The calculation from volumes of CO_2 to pressure is rather complicated, so the best way to determine pressure is to use a chart. See the resources section (page 148) for a reference to one of the best charts available.

For this experiment, any plastic bottle of commercial soda will do. Try to match the size of the bottle to an amount just under the capability of the scale. Bigger bottles will show more CO_2 escaping overall, so it will be easier to determine weight, but to have one that is beyond the capacity of the scale will not help at all. Depending on the size of the bottle, the CO_2 loss is likely to be between 2 and 15 g, so choose a scale with appropriate precision. A can could be used, but the bottle is easier to decarbonate because of the resealable lid. This experiment works well at room temperature so that the soda will decarbonate more quickly.

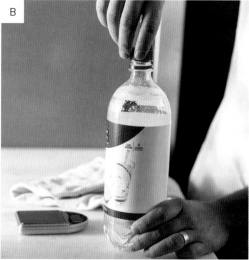

MATERIALS

Scale that will measure in grams

Bottle of commercial soda

Notebook to record weights

PROCEDURE

1. Weigh the full unopened bottle of soda and record the weight in grams. **(A)**

2. Carefully loosen the lid to allow gas to escape, but be sure all the drops of liquid stay in the plastic bottle for accurate measurements. **(B)**

3. Squeeze the bottle to eliminate headspace while sealing the lid back up. Shake vigorously until the bottle repressurizes. If it does repressurize, repeat steps 1 through 3. If it does not, move on to step 4.

4. Record the final weight of the decarbonated beverage. Depending on the size of the bottle, there should be a difference of probably a few grams. **(C)**

5. Take the difference of the two weights to determine total CO_2 loss.

6. Divide CO_2 loss (in grams) by the volume held in the bottle (in liters). Example: 12-ounce bottle (355 ml) with 2.4 g CO_2 loss should be 2.4 g ÷ 0.355 L = 6.76 g/L. 1 volume is equal to 1.96 g/L, so 6.76 g/L ÷ 1.96 g/L = 3.44 volumes.

7. Check a carbonation/volumes chart to determine what pressure is required to hold that much CO_2 in solution at room temperature. Zahm & Nagel (see Resources, page 148) has an accessible CO_2 solubility chart that has a wider temperature and pressure range than most charts available.

SCIENCE FAIR EXTRA CREDIT

Here are some additional ideas to getting the most out of this experiment as a science project, just for fun:

1. Considering the pressure in an average soda can/bottle, use the chart to determine what the pressure would be on the shelf at the store (about 70°F, or 21°C), in the refrigerator (about 35°F, or 2°C), or left in the car on a hot summer day (about 105°F, or 41°C).

2. How do the pressures of different flavors compare? How do the same flavors of different brands compare? How do multiple cans/bottles of the same flavor from the same brand compare?

3. Record the number of times it takes to release pressure from the bottle. Is there a difference between diet and regular flavors of the same brand? What does this suggest about the stability of carbonation in the presence of sugar?

CARBONATION METHODS

One thing that led me here was trying to get the most possible carbonation into my homemade creations. I started using dry ice, but it never quite got to a carbonation level that I was satisfied with. It bubbled all over the place, usually splashing out of the container. I knew I needed it colder, but sometimes it would get to a point where the dry ice would freeze the liquid directly around it and create a somewhat insulating protective shell of ice, and the bubbling would slow to a crawl. At one point, I opted to use club soda on top of syrup, but without careful handling I often lost a lot of carbonation. I prefer to use my own carbonated water on top of syrup as the easiest method with the most carbonation, provided that I'm careful to not jostle it too much. I have never been much a fan of fermentation with its inherent yeasty taste and volatility. For various reasons, it took me a fair amount of research before I was quite comfortable with trying fermentation, even though it's a bit more laissez-faire, so to speak. But when I got to it, I found the carbonation level can be quite satisfying.

This experiment is designed to help identify personal preference for carbonation level as well as illustrate the relative ease or difficulty between methods. Combining this with the previous pressure experiment will give an idea of the ranges of carbonation achievable by various methods.

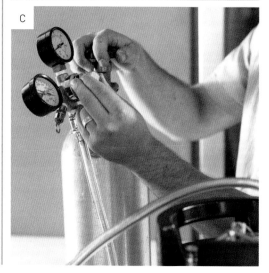

MATERIALS

Keg setup, soda siphon, or home carbonator, with
    water to fill it

8 ounces (225 g) dry ice

3 (2 L, or ½ gallon) plastic soda bottles

¼ cup (50 g) sugar

⅛ teaspoon active dry yeast

1½ gallons (6 L) water

FERMENTATION PROCEDURE (A)

1. Mix the sugar into 2 L (½ gallon) of room temperature water and add to one of the bottles.

2. Hydrate the yeast in ¼ cup (60 ml) of warm water. When it has started to foam, add it to the bottle and seal it.

3. Allow to ferment for 12 to 36 hours or until the bottle has firmed up completely.

DRY ICE PROCEDURE (B)

1. Fill the second bottle with 2 L (½ gallon) of chilled water.

2. Carefully break up the dry ice so it will fit into the bottle. Be sure to use proper safety equipment to avoid frostbite.

3. Feed small amounts of dry ice at a time into the mouth of the bottle and let them bubble away as they absorb into the water. Feeding them in all at once will cause it to bubble over out of the bottle.

4. When all the dry ice has been fed into the bottle and the bubbling has subsided, the cap can be sealed just before the last tiny bits of dry ice have disappeared. Do not try to seal it with any more than a few pea-size bits of dry ice as it has the potential to explode.

KEG/SIPHON PROCEDURE (C)

1. Fill a clean, sanitized keg with 4 to 5 gallons (15.2 to 19 L) of chilled water and seal the lid.

2. Hook up the CO_2 disconnect, turn on the CO_2, and set the regulator to 30 to 40 psi.

3. Shake the keg vigorously until the pressure gauge no longer moves on the dial as the keg shakes.

4. Allow the keg to settle for an hour or so for everything to get fully equilibrated.

5. Using a picnic tap, carefully fill the third bottle and seal it.

6. If using a siphon, fill and charge according to the manufacturer's recommendations instead of using the 2-liter bottle.

COMPARISONS

1. When all 3 bottles are fully carbonated, place the bottles in the refrigerator for at least 1 hour.

2. Pour glasses of each and compare the perceived level of carbonation.

3. For further comparison, follow the procedure for the previous experiment to calculate and compare carbonation levels based on volumes of CO_2.

ACIDITY

The proper balance of acidity can significantly affect the flavor and the safety of homemade soda. A low pH does not always impart a sour or tart flavor, but that's usually the case, especially among the ingredients used for soda making. Being able to relate a general pH level to a given level of tartness can serve as a reference point for other ingredients or properties.

Having the proper pH is extremely important for any recipes that use vegetables. Vegetables usually have a higher pH than fruits, and many are grown in the dirt, where serious contamination can occur. A pH of 4.6 or higher leaves the possibility of botulism growth. Generally, carbonated water by itself is down around 4.3, so that's usually safe. When carbonating ready-to-drink options that contain vegetables or vegetable juice, particularly in a keg, refrigerating the beverage as it's carbonating is a wise decision.

For fermentation, be sure that the mix's pH is below 4.6 before adding the yeast so that nothing unexpected and dangerous will grow alongside it.

Quick pH measurement can be done with a meter to give more exacting measurements or by using pH test strips that change color. The meter is nice because it spits out a number without much other work. Keep in mind, though, that these need calibration from time to time and must be stored in a manner that will preserve the electrodes, such as in buffer solution or distilled water. Many pH meters have very fragile electrodes and need to be handled with care.

Test strips are inexpensive, but sometimes it can be difficult to pinpoint the pH with much precision. Matching the color of the strip to the standards given is not always as straightforward as it might seem.

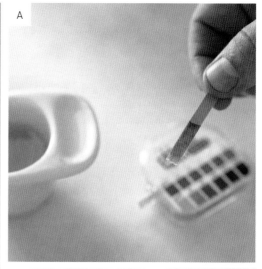

MATERIALS

pH test strips (available online through laboratory supply shops)

pH meter (available through online retailers)

3 or 4 different test solutions—a commercial soda and a homemade soda would be good comparisons. Lemon juice and carrot juice would also give a broad range of different pH levels and flavors.

Sample cups—2-ounce (60 ml) drinking cups or 1-ounce (30-ml) soufflé cups work well.

Eye dropper or pipette

Distilled water for rinsing

PROCEDURE

1. Pour test solutions into sample cups.

2. For the test strips, use an eye dropper or pipette to dab a drop of solution onto the test paper. **(A)** It should turn colors instantly. Rinse the pipette between samples.

3. Compare the strip to the color standard supplied with the strips to determine the pH.

4. For the pH meter, be sure that the meter is calibrated according to the manufacturer's instructions.

5. Dip the probe directly into the sample cup and wait for the instrument to stabilize. **(B)** It should have a fairly quick digital display that gives a pH reading to at least the nearest tenths decimal.

SCIENCE FAIR EXTRA CREDIT

Here are some additional ideas to getting the most out of this experiment as a science project, just for fun:

1. Compare sodas with similar pH values. What ingredients stand out as acids?

2. Many acids as ingredients are buffered. A buffer system includes a compound with the acid's negative ion, such as citric acid and sodium citrate. Which samples have a buffer in the ingredient list?

3. Find a sample that is buffered and one that is not that have a similar pH. Add a small amount of baking soda and check the pH again. How do they compare?

FLAVOR EXTRACTION

Sometimes adding a very flavorful ingredient to a recipe does not produce the expected results. Vanilla is one of these ingredients that seem like they should have more flavor to contribute than expected. In reality, it does; it's just harder to draw out than most other flavor ingredients used in soda making. Flavors can be oil soluble, water soluble, or somewhere in between. Flavor extraction is a great way of drawing out flavors that don't emerge well with steeping. Alcohol is commonly used in flavor extraction because it can be a solvent to dissolve some oil-soluble compounds and it will also dissolve as a solute in water. To understand the capabilities and limitations of flavor extraction, a quality vanilla extract can be made at home with only a few ingredients. Other flavoring components, such as mint, can also be used to make extracts for different flavors using the same methods. Try other ingredients to get a feel for what flavors work best as steeped flavors and which do better as extracts.

Pure vanilla extract has a standard of 35% alcohol. Using this information, a high-proof, neutral flavored alcohol can be utilized for that component. This extract has no more alcohol than a pure vanilla extract off the shelf, and it can be used in the same way. This is likely to have actual seeds in it as well, to add that artisanal vanilla bean look.

MATERIALS

Vanilla beans (about 14 beans for 2½ cups, or 570 ml, of extract)

151-proof (75% ABV) grain alcohol (or the highest proof vodka available)

Sealable bottle

Water

PROCEDURE

1. Split the vanilla beans and scrape the seeds. **(A)**

2. In the bottle, mix 9 ounces (250 ml) alcohol with 11 ounces (310 ml) water to bring the mix to 35% ABV. **(B)** Sometimes this can cause the extract to go cloudy and is normal. Using a 70- or 80-proof spirit is also an option, as it would require no mixing and is less likely to cloud.

3. Place the beans and seeds inside the bottle, seal, and shake. The liquid will start taking on the color of the beans immediately, but they will need to sit in the bottle for at least 3 to 8 weeks before they take on full flavor. **(C)** If it does go cloudy, this usually happens when alcohol is added first and dissolves oils that are not as soluble when alcohol is brought down to 35%.

SCIENCE OF SODA

Alcohol was used in some early soda flavors as an emulsifier for flavor oils to keep them in solution. Some supposed formulas for early versions of the big soda flavors of today have popped up here and there in recent years and they all list alcohol as one of the ingredients. Alcohol is a great solvent for flavors, and it is still used for the same purpose today. Check the extract bottles in the baking aisle and some will list the alcohol percentage in the ingredients.

SCIENCE OF SODA

While a number of websites list instructions for homemade extracts, a young child getting his or her hands on high proof alcohol is likely to turn a few heads. Be careful with this one if submitting to a science fair. It may be wise to request permission beforehand.

BRIX

Brix is a measure of dissolved solids; in most cases, those are sugars. It's measured using a refractometer by refractive index, meaning to what extent light will bend when it passes through the medium. A refractometer is a handy tool when determining sugar concentrations. It can also be used when determining specific gravity before fermentation, and some refractometers have a built-in specific gravity scale instead of having to convert from Brix with a calculation. In soda making, understanding relative sugar contents is helpful when developing recipes, particularly for the health conscious. When using juice concentrates for a recipe, it can be easy to forget that they have a relatively high sugar content already and then to get carried away using them only for flavor. Then the sugar content of the finished homemade beverage can be well above what a commercial soda might have.

Using a refractometer is as simple as applying a couple of drops of sugar solution to the prism, flipping the cover down, and looking through the eyepiece. Refractive index can change with temperature, so many refractometers have either a recommended temperature range or a temperature compensation feature. If most readings are taken with room temperature solution, they should be accurate.

Knowing the Brix and pH together help get the flavor spot-on and consistent from batch to batch. The Brix-to-acid ratio is actually what's used to determine ripeness of oranges and grades of orange juice. Too sweet and not enough sour will result in a syrupy taste, while too sour and not enough sweet will result in an unripened taste. Either scenario will yield a less appetizing soda than getting the correct ratio, which can vary for different flavors.

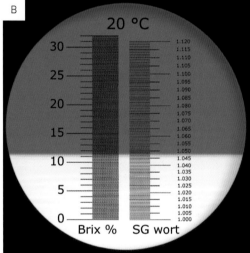

MATERIALS

3 to 5 different fruit juices—grapefruit, grape, apple, and lemon are good options for a wide range.

2 or 3 different commercial sodas—comparing diet soda to regular soda gives good results, as well as comparing cola to root beer, caffeinated citrus soda, and lemon-lime flavors.

2 or 3 homemade sodas

Handheld refractometer—these can range in price from $25 to over $200. An inexpensive model would do just fine for this job. A local university or vintner may have one that can be borrowed or rented for a small fee.

Lens cloth for cleaning the prism

Eyedropper or pipette

PROCEDURE

1. Prep the refractometer according to manufacturer's directions to check the calibration. This is usually done with distilled water to ensure that the refractometer reads at zero.

2. Place 2 or 3 drops of the solution to be measured onto the prism. **(A)** This is best done with an eyedropper or pipette.

3. Carefully close the cover over the prism so the solution spreads in a thin film. There should be no bubbles in solution after the prism is closed. If there are, open the cover and apply a few more drops.

4. Looking through the eyepiece, note where the line falls on the viewfinder field and record the °Brix. **(B)**

5. Repeat the procedure for all samples and compare the results.

SCIENCE FAIR EXTRA CREDIT

Brix does not measure sugar content, but does measure total dissolved solids. If nutrition labels are available for the samples obtained, compare the sugar content on the label to the measured Brix level.

1. Rank the samples according to Brix level and then separately according to sugar content from the nutrition label.

2. Compare the rankings to see if they are correct. If there are differences, what might cause the discrepancy? What might be some of the other dissolved solids?

3. Which samples match the nutrition labels the closest?

RESOURCES

These are some of the best places to find more information on the topic of homemade soda, to purchase ingredients and equipment, or to get otherwise involved.

SUPPLIES AND INGREDIENTS

CHI Company
www.chicompany.net
The CHI Company supplies to the beer, wine, soda, and vending industries. They also sell to individuals and often have used equipment. Their shipping prices and delivery times are not bad, and they have hard-to-find parts that don't usually show up in other places. I was able to find some reasonably priced parts to rebuild some used draft faucets that I had purchased. They also sell new ball lock–style kegs in various sizes that are hard to find elsewhere.

Midwest Homebrewing and Winemaking Supplies
www.midwestsupplies.com
This is one of the bigger home-brew stores in the United States. I purchased my first sets of equipment here, including bottles and a bottle capper, and my keg system. They are very knowledgeable and happy to answer questions as well. Keep on the lookout for occasional specials posted on their Facebook and Twitter feeds in addition to their homepage.

Austin Homebrew Supply
www.austinhomebrew.com
Another big home-brew supply house, Austin has a Web store that's very easy to navigate and offers pretty much flat rate shipping.

Northern Brewer
www.northernbrewer.com
Northern Brewer is more than just a supply store: They have an extensive information base on brewing beer along with an active forum. Among all the information on beer, some of which can be applied to soda making, there is some information and a few threads in the forum specific to soda.

Kegconnection
www.kegconnection.com
This is another supply store specializing in kegging systems. Feedback from people on the forums is that they are very reliable. Their prices and shipping are decent, and they do custom kit orders fully assembled.

Micro Matic
www.micromatic.com
Dedicated to draft beer dispensing, Micro Matic sells prebuilt kegerators and jockey boxes along with numerous parts for draft serving. They sell to individuals under the Home & Bar section. They also have a forum that welcomes both home users and commercial users.

SodaStream
www.sodastreamusa.com
If there isn't enough advertising about this in the local big box store, here is the place with the most information, including where to buy locally or at an online store. There are a lot of people who absolutely love their machine.

Monterey Bay Spice Co.
www.herbco.com
Can't find a sassafras tree to dig roots from? Worried about digging up the wrong thing? Ordering online is a great alternative. Anywhere that sells bulk herbs will likely have some, but I've found that Monterey Bay seems to have the best prices and biggest selection.

Prairie Moon Beverage Syrup
www.prairiemoon.biz
When looking for syrups or syrup concentrates, this company has some great flavors. The nice thing about the syrup concentrates is that they contain just flavor, not the sugar or water that's readily available and can be added according to taste. Considering shipping price and weight, the savings are excellent. They also have an extensive selection of soda siphons and offer advice on how to use them.

LorAnn Oils
www.lorannoils.com
LorAnn sells food-grade flavor oils labeled as Super Strength Flavors. Some are natural, some are artificial, and some are a blend. Sold for hard candies, these work great in emulsion recipes.

Amazon
www.amazon.com or
eBay
www.ebay.com
These are great places to look for equipment. Anything from ingredients to pH papers can be found here for very reasonable prices. For equipment, keep in mind that there is a wide range of quality available from these sites, so be careful when buying any precision equipment. Pay attention to reviews and consider the location that the items are coming from as well as the purpose for which the equipment is to be used. Anything that requires an exact measurement is worth paying extra for. Anything that is just a nice-to-have item or something that you need for a relative or ballpark measurement is fine to buy on the inexpensive side.

BOOKS

Homemade Soda
by Andrew Schloss
With 200 recipes and tips on making homemade soda, this book is similar to Cresswell's book (see below) but includes tips on more methods for carbonation, more types of recipes, and more recipes in general. Most are scaled to a 12-ounce (355 ml) serving but can easily be scaled up.

Make Your Own Soda: Syrup Recipes
by Anton Nocito
This book contains artisan syrup recipes by the founder of P&H Soda. It has a number of solid recipes, from fountain classics to gourmet creations, with an artisanal flair. Nocito specializes in using natural, fresh ingredients, and his recipes are created accordingly.

Cordials from Your Kitchen
by Pattie Vargas and Rich Gulling
Although mostly focused on homemade liqueurs, this is an excellent source for flavor inspiration, and some of the information is applicable to making homemade extracts.

Homemade Root Beer, Soda & Pop
by Stephen Cresswell
This is a great reference full of historical tidbits and recipes, including a bit about tapping maple and birch trees for sap. It contains mostly fermented recipes, with instructions on adaptation for force carbonation.

The Artisan Soda Workshop
by Andrea Lynn
This is a small book, specifically designed with the SodaStream in mind. It contains great artisanal flavor combinations, but expect some of the ingredients to have artisanal prices. It is a great reference for those looking to develop their own SodaStream recipes.

True Brews
by Emma Christensen
This book is dedicated to the merits of fermented beverages. If a beverage is or can be fermented, chances are it'll be in here. Emma Christensen writes for The Kitchn and has been a beer reviewer for other publications. Among the many recipes it contains, it has a basic soda recipe and technique that Christensen builds off of with a few variations on flavor.

The Art of Fermentation
by Sandor Ellix Katz
This is a hefty reference for all things fermented, including a number of interesting soda recipes. Most are not easily adapted to force carbonation, but it's not out of the question. It is mostly a reference for technique, as the recipes are not always precise.

Fix the Pumps
by Darcy O'Neil
Written by the author of the Art of Drink blog, this focuses on the history of the soda fountain and contains mostly cocktail recipes, but it also contains some good information on soda making.

FORUMS AND BLOGS

Home Brew Talk Forum

www.homebrewtalk.com
This is probably the biggest home-brew forum on the Internet today. They have an extensive user base, and some really great recipes are regularly submitted to their soda section.

Northern Brewer Homebrew Forum

forum.northrenbrewer.com
One of the only forums set up by a supply store, this is mostly about brewing beer, but someone occasionally brings up questions about soda.

Brew Plus Forums

www.brewplus.com/forum
This is another home-brew forum, but they have a soda forum as well. It is not as active as HomeBrewTalk, and without as much content, but is growing.

Art of Drink

www.artofdrink.com
Although a blog mostly about cocktails, it has a nice section with soda history and some recipe ideas, mostly striving to re-create Coke. All in all, it is a fascinating read with links to purchase hard-to-find ingredients like acid phosphate.

Ellen's Kitchen

www.ellenskitchen.com
My recipes are mostly in 1-gallon (3.8 liter) yields, which is a bit much if making a recipe for just one person or a bit small if making it for a gathering. Ellen's Kitchen has a lot of great information for planning for a large group. It has recipes, estimates for large gatherings, and even a forum for recipe requests.

Emma E. Christensen

emmaelizabethchristensen.blogspot.com
Christensen edits recipes for The Kitchn and offers up advice on all things fermented. Her blog isn't frequently updated, but it's not bad. Catch her there or at The Kitchn itself: www.thekitchn.com

The Homemade Soda Expert

homemadesodaexpert.blogspot.com
This is my own blog, where you can find a handful more recipes, book reviews, and answers to questions. Stop by sometime and drop me a line.

TECHNICAL INFORMATION

Lancer Corporation

www.lancercorp.com
Lancer is a manufacturer of post-mix soda systems. Finding a used system is not difficult, though maintaining it might require some know-how. Lancer has a downloadable PowerPoint file in their Technical Documents section that is an excellent overview of how post-mix systems work.

Zahm & Nagel

www.zahmnagel.com
Zahm & Nagel is a company that specializes in CO_2 testing equipment for the food industry. They have a wider range CO_2 volumes chart that is available as a pdf, though the link is difficult to find. The link to the chart is on the product page for both of their Series 6000 and Series 7000 products. Unlike many of the charts that are specific to beer styles, this chart has a temperature range from 32° to 100°F (0 to 38°C) and a pressure range from 0 to 100 psi.

FAQ ABOUT SODA

I have an open "ask the expert" policy on my blog, and while I'm more than happy to answer questions individually, here are some of the ones that I see come back up every now and again.

I have a ginger beer recipe that requires ginger bug or ginger beer plant. Is that necessary? Where can I get some?

Ginger bug or ginger beer plant is a symbiotic colony of bacteria and yeasts (or SCOBY) used to ferment a ginger beer. The recipe will work just as well with a champagne yeast but the flavor may come out differently. Traditionally it is fermented in an open vessel to make a more alcoholic version of ginger beer rather than just a soda. To differentiate, a ginger bug is a starter culture made from scratch. Ginger beer plant is a SCOBY that has been perpetuated for some number of years and is divided and traded or sold the world over like a vinegar mother. A brief internet search will usually turn up someone willing to sell some.

How do I start bottling and selling my homemade soda?

The answer to this question varies depending on location. In the U.S., it is regulated by individual states but it usually involves having the local health department inspect the kitchen in which the soda will be made, storing ingredients separate from ingredients for personal use, ensuring that no children or pets are present during the making of soda intended for sale, and the proper licensing and insurance required by the locale. Check with the local health department to see what is required.

Depending on the recipe, it may also be possible to have a small production run by a bottler that can handle the proper ingredients, but such a course could easily require an investment of at least $10,000 for 500 to 700 cases of product.

Why do some recipes have cream of tartar? Is that necessary?

Cream of tartar is a great acid for inverting sugar but otherwise doesn't have much function in beverages. If a recipe calls for cream of tartar but doesn't list a significant boil time, it's likely that it doesn't necessarily need to be in there. It doesn't contribute body or do anything for head retention as some believe.

How much maltodextrin should I put in my soda?

Maltodextrin can come in so many different forms, and any one brand may vary quite significantly from any other. I've had some sodas that included maltodextrin that had the consistency of mud, while in other sodas it wasn't noticeable at all. When purchasing a maltodextrin from a homebrew store for head retention, it's safe to follow the guidelines provided. If obtaining a maltodextrin from another source, be sure to start out with small dosages and add more in small increments until the desired effect is achieved.

Why am I getting such inconsistent results?

Inconsistent results could be from technique or it could be based on inconsistent ingredients. Write down almost everything that happens and keep notes on even the things that sometimes seem insignificant. A faulty regulator may cause inconsistent pressures for a force carbonated system while even small temperature and pressure swings can affect the outcome. Many roots and herbs available commercially are still harvested from the wild, and while vendors strive for consistency and quality, natural ingredients will have some natural variation.

If I'm bottling sodas, how long will the carbonation last?

As long as the bottle is properly sealed, the carbonation should last indefinitely. It should last at least as long or longer than the soda's normal shelf life. It can sometimes seem like bottled sodas from a force carbonated system tend to lose carbonation, but this is simply to pressurize the headspace; once that happens, it should remain the same until opened.

How do I make flavored soda waters without sweeteners?

It may seem as if just leaving out the sweetener in any recipe should make a tasty flavored seltzer. Unfortunately, that's not always the case. Sweeteners can sometimes mask off flavors or change how some flavors are manifested. The simplest way to do a flavored soda water is to add just a little bit of juice to it; another route is to use flavor oils. The end result will depend greatly on the flavoring and personal preference and will likely require some trial and error.

What sanitizers do you recommend?

I like to use bleach solution on bottles that I don't intend to ferment. It's quick, cheap, and it's effective. On stainless steel or in fermented recipes, an acid based sanitizer is usually the best option.

How can I get my cola to taste more like one of the major brands?

Many people are surprised to hear that the phosphoric acid is a strong contributor to flavor. Getting ahold of it can be difficult, though. Another difference in my opinion is that the red cola tends to be less sweet and have more spice flavor to it while the blue cola tends to be sweeter and has more of a fruity flavor from a higher percentage of citric acid.

I tried adding your syrups to my SodaStream bottle and it foamed over like a volcano. What happened?

SodaStream syrups are designed with an artificial sweetener to optimize carbonated water to syrup ratio. This allows the syrups to be more compact without a huge increase in sugar concentration. At a high concentration, sugar will knock CO_2 out of solution and can start to bubble over. Try using stevia along with real sugar to get a closer approximation of how well the SodaStream's commercial syrups mix with the carbonated water without compromising sweetness or carbonation. It's also a good idea to keep everything as cold as possible and mix carefully. I prefer to add syrup to the bottom of the bottle first and then top off with carbonated water. This requires an extra bottle and is a little bit more work, but it keeps the mixing and surface contact between syrup and seltzer to a minimum until the bottle is sealed.

SODA FOR THE HOMEBREWER

For many home beer brewers, homemade soda is something that is easily understood and mastered so long as some differences between beer brewing and soda making are clearly addressed. I see some common myths that pop up from time to time on the homebrew forums from people that are looking to share their homebrewing hobby with others who don't drink beer.

Here are some of the more frequent ones in no particular order:

Fermented soda won't contain any alcohol.

Fermentation always creates alcohol. A highly carbonated soda will have about 0.5% to 0.7% ABV. It's not much in terms of alcoholic beverages, but the legal cut-off between alcoholic and non-alcoholic is 0.5%. Alcohol content is measurable with a hydrometer. If making soda for someone particularly sensitive to alcohol, it might be best to go another route.

Fermenting soda in glass bottles will cause them to explode.

It is possible to ferment a soda in a glass bottle without exploding, but it either must be vigilantly monitored or a non-fermentable sweetener must be used with only enough sugar to carbonate. There are kits available that use stevia or sucralose to sweeten and sugar or dextrose as yeast food to carbonate.

Kegged soda filled into glass bottles will go flat.

A counterpressure filler to control foaming and turbulence will work wonders. Any sealed carbonated drink will only lose enough carbonation to pressurize the headspace to equilibrium; for this reason, larger bottles will hold carbonation better than smaller bottles.

Soda can't be served from a beer faucet.

A stainless steel (not chrome or brass) draft faucet is fine for soda if there is either enough line to balance the high psi or another form of pressure compensation in the system, such as a flow control valve. Seals within a faucet may hold on to some stronger flavors, but with a good cleaning they should come out just fine.

Soda needs dedicated kegs.

Used "homebrew" kegs held soda once, so while some of the strong flavors such as root beer or cola may be tough to remove, it's not impossible. Keep an extra set of O-rings specifically for root beer or cola if it becomes a problem. It might also help to have a dedicated beverage line. Time is a critical factor; if the keg is carbonated and served in a short period of time, a good cleaning should get rid of the smell. Fill the keg and line with water and store for about a week to help remove any stubborn flavors.

ACKNOWLEDGMENTS

This book would not have been possible without a number of people. It seems fitting to mention them here, though I'm not sure a mere mention even does their kindness justice. Moreover, there are so many others who simply won't fit on these pages. So I'm just gonna crack open a soda and drink to all the people who have helped me get to this point.

To Jonathan Simcosky and everyone else at Quarry: Thank you for this wonderful opportunity and for putting up with my tardiness. I appreciate your understanding and help along the way.

To my dear wife, Shana, who has put up with syrup spilled into the stove and ridiculous numbers of bottles cluttering the fridge, has endured an empty bed with late nights while I refurbished a vintage fridge in the basement to hold the extras, has offered kindness and understanding when it died two weeks later, has taste-tested the worst of my failures, and has been so supportive of my hobby even though she has no interest in carbonation. Thank you for all that you are and everything you do! I love you!

Thank you to my dear children, who are brutally honest in their evaluation of my flavors. Who knew that being picky eaters would be so ever important in recipe development?

To Paul and Dana Sobota: Your genius photography and styling has really made this book come alive beyond anything I ever imagined.

Thank you to Jim Kittle, who encouraged me in my writing and for treating a pupil as a peer.

Thank you to all my friends, mentors, and colleagues at the BYU food science department, particularly Lynn Ogden, who shares my admiration for all things carbonated.

To everyone who has been willing to taste even my strangest creations at family gatherings and church picnics: I thank you for your honest feedback and for pushing me to make more.

To Mom, Dad, Dave, Tiffany, and Marissa: Thanks for helping make me what I am today and for always being supportive. I hope I can make you all as proud of me as I am to count myself among you as family. And thanks, Mom, for rarely discouraging me from playing with my food.

To my late friend Bradley and his dear wife, Kate. Thank you, Brad, for pointing me down the road to food science. Both of you have influenced the two most important decisions of my life, and I only wish we could all share in this success together. It is every bit your doing as it is mine.

To the rest of the Allen family, who have been as supportive to me as they have been to their own sons. Thank you for letting me be a part of your home on a nearly regular basis.

And last but not least, thanks to you, the reader, whether you came to this book by way of my Homemade Soda Expert blog or whether this book has led you to my blog. Thank you for being a part of it and joining in the journey. This drink's for you. Enjoy!

ABOUT THE AUTHOR

Jeremy Butler is a trained food scientist, having earned a B.S. in food science from Brigham Young University. Playing with food has been a big part of his life from an early age. His love of bubbly beverages comes from his highly influential high school years, which tasted mostly like the Jones Soda Co.'s Pink, Fufu Berry, Green Apple, and Cream sodas. Currently he does product development for a contract manufacturer in the frozen foods industry. He has taken upon himself the title of Self-Proclaimed Expert in the fast-growing field of homemade soda. In his 10 or so minutes of spare time between work, loving his family, attending to church callings, and sleeping, he creates and posts recipes on his blog, The Homemade Soda Expert, and answers soda-related questions on the HomeBrewTalk Forums under the more humble moniker of MrFoodScientist. Drop him a line at homemadesodaexpert@gmail.com or follow him on Twitter @HomeSodaExpert.

INDEX